ENCORE

ENCORE

Prize Poems
2020

Editor
Kathy Lohrum Cotton

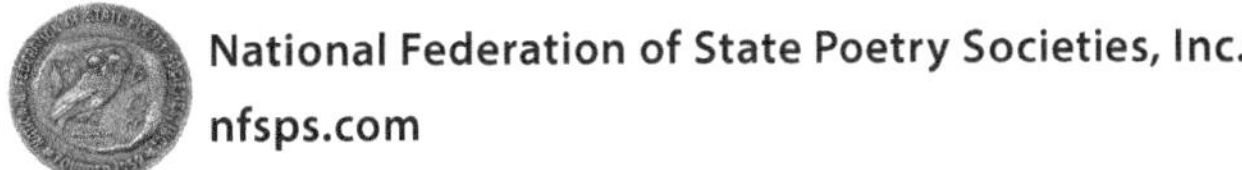

National Federation of State Poetry Societies, Inc.
nfsps.com

Encore Prize Poems 2020

© 2020 as a collection by the National Federation of State Poetry Societies, Inc. (NFSPS), with first rights only. All rights to individual poems remain with the contributing poets. No part of this work may be reproduced or transmitted in any form or by any means, electronic or mechanical, or by use of any information storage or retrieval system, except as may be expressly permitted by the individual poet. We ask that credit be given to NFSPS when reprinting is granted. Individual authors confirm that these poems are their original creations, and to the publisher's knowledge these poems were written by the listed poets. NFSPS does not guarantee nor assume responsibility for verifying the authorship of each work.

Published July 2020
National Federation of State Poetry Societies, Inc.
nfsps.com

Edit and design by Kathy Lohrum Cotton
Set in Minion Pro Medium and Myriad Pro Condensed

Cover photo by Steve Halama
NFSPS Medallion, David Nufer Photography
Title with permission of Alice Briley, Past President, NFSPS

ISBN: 9798663013383
Independently published

Printed in the United States of America

NFSPS, organized in 1959, now umbrellas 32 state poetry societies. The Federation is a non-profit organization, exclusively educational and literary and dedicated to the furtherance of poetry on the national level. It annually sponsors:

- **Fifty poetry contests (three student contests added in 2020)** with cash prizes totaling more than $8,000, including a grand prize of $1,000, plus publication of each contest's top-three winning poems in the annual *Encore* anthology.

- **The Stevens Poetry Manuscript Competition** for a single author's collection of poems, with a cash prize of $1,000, plus publication and 50 copies of the book.

- **The College Undergraduate Poetry (CUP) Competition** with two awards, the Meudt Memorial and Kahn Memorial, each offering a $500 prize, plus chapbook publication, 75 copies, and convention travel stipends.

- **The BlackBerryPeach Prizes for Poetry: Spoken & Heard,** a performance poetry competition, awards three prizes—first place $1,000, second $500, and third $250, plus chapbook publication, performance video posting on YouTube, and convention travel stipends.

- **The Manningham Trust Student Poetry Contest** which includes a junior division for grades 6–8 and senior division for grades 9–12. The top ten poems in each division at state-level competitions advance to the national contest. The top ten national winners in each division win cash prizes and publication in Manningham's annual anthology.

- **A national poetry convention,** hosted by a member state society, with poetry workshops, speakers, panel discussions, presentation of awards to contest winners, open-mic readings, and entertainment. The 2020 convention was canceled due to the coronavirus pandemic.

For further information, visit nfsps.com.

HONORARY CHANCELLORS

1960 Joseph Auslander
1962 John Crowe Ransom
1963 Glenn Ward Dresbach
1964 Jesse Stuart
1965 Grace Noll Crowell
1966 Jean Starr Untermeyer
1968 Loring Williams
1969 Harry M. Meachum
1970 John Williams Andrews
1971 August Derleth
1972 William E. Stafford
1973 N. Scott Momaday

1974 Richard Armour
1975 Richard Eberhart
1976 James Dickey
1977 Judson Jerome
1979 John Ciardi
1981 Robert Coles
1983 Richard Shelton
1985 Marcia Lee Masters
1986 Robert Penn Warren
1987 Richard Wilber
1990 William E. Stafford
1992 Rodney Jones

1995 Tess Gallagher
1997 Michael Bugeja
2000 David Wagoner
2002 Maxine Kumin
2004 Naomi Shihab Nye
2006 Li Young Lee
2008 Lewis Turco
2010 Ted Kooser
2012 Natasha Trethewey
2015 Peter Meinke
2018 Jo McDougall
2019 David Rothman

NFSPS PRESIDENTS

1959–1960	Cecilia Parsons Miller*	Pennsylvania Poetry Society
1960–1961	Clinton F. Larson*	Utah State Poetry Society
1961–1962	Robert D. West*	Ohio State Poetry Society
1962–1964	Edna Meudt*	Wisconsin Fellowship of Poets
1964–1966	Marvin Davis Winsett*	Poetry Society of Texas
1966–1968	Max C. Golightly*	Utah State Poetry Society
1968–1970	Hans Juergensen*	West Virginia Poetry Society
1970–1972	Russell Ferrall*	Wisconsin Fellowship of Poets
1972–1974	Jean Jenkins*	Utah State Poetry Society
1974–1976	Catherine Case Lubbe*	Poetry Society of Texas
1976–1978	Glenn Robert Swetman	Louisiana State Poetry Society
1978–1979	Carl P. Morton*	Alabama State Poetry Society
1979–1981	Alice Briley*	New Mexico State Poetry Society
1981–1983	Wauneta Hackleman*	Arizona State Poetry Society
1983–1885	Jack E. Murphy*	Poetry Society of Texas
1985–1987	Barbara Stevens*	South Dakota State Poetry Society
1987–1988	Henrietta A. Kroah*	Florida State Poets Association, Inc.
1988–1990	Jerry Robbins*	Kentucky State Poetry Society
1990–1992	Pat Stodghill	Poetry Society of Texas
1992–1994	Wanda B. Blaisdell*	Utah State Poetry Society
1994–1996	Ralph Hammond	Alabama State Poetry Society
1996–1998	Amy Jo Zook	Verse Writers Guild of Ohio
1998–2000	Susan Stevens Chambers	League of Minnesota Poets
2000–2002	Clarence P. Socwell*	Utah State Poetry Society
2002–2004	Madelyn Eastlund	Florida State Poets Association, Inc.
2004–2006	Budd Powell Mahan	Poetry Society of Texas
2006–2008	Doris Stengel	League of Minnesota Poets
2008–2010	Nancy Baass	Poetry Society of Texas
2010–2012	Russell H. Strauss	Poetry Society of Tennessee
2012–2014	Jeremy Downes	Alabama State Poetry Society
2014–2016	Eleanor Berry	Oregon Poetry Association
2016–2018	Jim Barton*	Poets' Roundtable of Arkansas
2018–2020	Julie Cummings	Columbine Poets of Colorado

*Deceased

EXECUTIVE BOARD

President: Membership Coordinator, Publicity Chair Electronic Media .... Julie Cummings   CO

1st Vice President: *Strophes* Editor, Electronic Media Assistant ....Paul Ford   UT

2nd Vice President: Development Chair (Endowments, Sponsorships),

    BlackBerryPeach Prizes for Poetry Chair ....Joseph Cavanaugh   FL

3rd Vice President: Special Awards Chair .... Charmaine Pappas Donovan   MN

4th Vice President: College Undergraduate Poetry Competition Chair,

    Contest Sponsors /Brochure Co-Chair ....Steven Concert   PA

Chancellor: Convention Coordinator ....Polly Opsahl   MI

1st Vice Chancellor: Judges Chair..JoAn Howerton   TN

2nd Vice Chancellor .... Loretta Diane Walker   TX

Treasurer .... Linda Harris   IA

Secretary.. Jessica Temple   AL

Immediate Past President/Presidential Advisors Chair ....Eleanor Berry   OR

APPOINTIVE BOARD

Board Liaison to State Societies ....Russell H. Strauss   TN

Contest Chair ....Carla Jordan   CO

Convention Coordinator ....Polly Opsahl   MI

Encore Editor ....Kathy Lohrum Cotton   IL

Historian ....Nancy Baass   TX

Legal Counselor, Manningham Trust Competition Chair .... Susan Stevens Chambers   MN

Librarian .... Catherine L'Herisson   TX

Manningham Trust Advisor .... Sam Wood   NV

Publicity Chair, Traditional Media and Poetry Day/Poetry Month Liaison Co-chair ....Amy Jo Zook   OH

Special Events / State Outreach ....Peter Stein   MN

Stevens Manuscript Competition Chair ....To be appointed   AR

Strophes Associate Editor... Jim Lambert   IL

Website .... Billy Pennington   OK

Youth Chair .... Rosemerry Wahtola Trommer   CO

1. NFSPS Founders Award
2. Winners' Circle Award
3. The NFSPS Board Award
4. The Margo Award
5. Donald Stodghill Memorial Award
6. Georgia Poetry Society Award
7. Stone Gathering Award
8. Poetry Society of Texas Award
9. Jim Barton, Bard of the Pines Award
10. Al Laster Memorial Award
11. Jim Barton Memorial Award
12. Alabama State Poetry Society Award
13. Land of Enchantment Award
14. Power of Women Award
15. The Virginia Corrie-Cozart Memorial Award
16. Arizona State Poetry Society Award
17. Mildred Vorpahl Baass Remembrance Award
18. League of Minnesota Poets Award
19. Jessica C. Saunders Memorial Award
20. Poetry Society of Indiana Award
21. Nevada Poetry Society Award
22. William Stafford Memorial Award
23. The New York Poetry Forum Award
24. Columbine Poets of Colorado Award
25. Morton D. Prouty & Elsie S. Prouty Memorial
26. Traditional Haiku Award
27. Louisiana State Poetry Society Award

28. Evelyn Corry Appelbee Memorial Award
29. Utah State Poetry Society Award
30. CSPS James E. MacWhinney Memorial Award
31. Illinois State Poetry Society Award
32. The Robbie Award
33. Ohio Award
34. Florida State Poets Association, Inc. Award
35. Poetry Society of Michigan Award
36. Mississippi Poetry Society Award
37. Jesse Stuart Memorial Award
38. Minute Award
39. Barbara Stevens Memorial Award
40. Alice Mackenzie Swaim Memorial Award
41. Poetry Society of Oklahoma Award
42. Save Our Earth Award
43. Massachusetts State Poetry Society Award
44. Poetry Society of Tennessee Award
45. Iowa Poetry Association Award
46. Wyopoets Award
47. San Antonio Poets Association Award
48. Maine Poets Society Award
49. Miriam S. Strauss Memorial Award
50. The Poets Northwest Award

Student Award (Grades 9–12)
Poetry in the Classroom Award (Grades 6–8)
Poetry in the Classroom Award (Grades 3–5)

CONTENTS

1. NFSPS FOUNDERS AWARD (to honor Mary B. Wall), sponsored by NFSPS, Inc.

Judge Jared Smith; Lafayette, CO

2. WINNERS' CIRCLE AWARD, sponsored by Diane Glancy, Harriet Stovall Kelley, Pat Stodghill and Pat Underwood (previous prize winners in Contest 1, NFSPS Founders Award)

Judge Jeremy Downes; Auburn, AL

3. THE NFSPS BOARD AWARD, sponsored by the NFSPS Executive and Appointive Boards

Judge Steven Concert; Harveys Lake, PA

4. THE MARGO AWARD, in memory of Margo LaGattuta, sponsored by her friends

Judge Barbara Funke; Valparaiso, IN

5. DONALD STODGHILL MEMORIAL AWARD, sponsored by Pat Stodghill

Judge Julie Cummings; Conifer, CO

6. GEORGIA POETRY SOCIETY AWARD, sponsored by the Georgia Poetry Society

Judge Jessica Temple; Huntsville, AL

CONTENTS

CONTENTS

CONTENTS

Encore 2020 arrives halfway through a bewildering year, with the worldwide Covid-19 pandemic, economic upheaval, and racial justice protests. We may long be weaving into poetry the challenging experiences of these times.

With the cancellation of our national convention, the 2020 contests' winning poems had no cheering audience for the announcements and readings. Instead, the 159 prize poems—chosen from more than 6,500 submissions by poets across the nation and from Canada, the United Kingdom and Spain—debut in this anthology.

Another first for us: added to our traditional 50 annual competitions are three student awards. Categories for high-school, middle-school and grade-school poets were offered with no entry fees.

You will find in this volume visually unique concrete/shape poems; fixed forms like pantoum, villanelle, and sonnet; and the short 3-line haiku, 13-line trimeric and 60-syllable minute poems. Beneath many titles, assigned forms are identified to help you appreciate the poets' constraints.

In two new contests about women—"Renaissance Woman" and "A Women's Authentic Power"—we give a nod to the century-anniversary celebration of women's suffrage. The collection also includes fresh, personal interpretations of themes as wide-ranging as wolves and hometown heroes, loss of a child and environmental issues, books and borders. Each contest's subject is listed above the poem so you can share some beginning points of our poets' inspirations.

Mark Terry of Orlando, Florida, opens the 2020 *Encore* with his $1,000 prize-winning poem, "The Secret Language of Ideas," while children from Colorado, Iowa and Kentucky close the collection. Between those pages lie sorrow and humor, wisdom and passion, and the uniqueness of many voices on many subjects. We invite you to explore cover-to-cover.

We also welcome you to learn more about the National Federation of State Poetry Societies and our 32 member state societies. Note the lists of our contests, publications and leadership, and for more information visit nfsps.com.

Kathy Lohrum Cotton, Editor
July 2020

First Place, Mark Terry, Orlando, FL

The Secret Language of Ideas

We know they're there by their clues,
patterns mostly, a mathematical puzzle,
like the way freshly-cut grass forms
into interlaced, unfamiliar runes—
suggestions, fragments of letters
in hues of ocher, lime and moss green,
chiding us to try and decipher.

It's like the way the piano keys sit
in their neatly ordered row, silently,
white and black, each a single tone,
that tone with infinite possibilities,
able to resonate into the lightest
and the darkest halls within—waiting
for a knowing touch, pleading to live.

It's like peering into a sauce pan
without a recipe to follow, just some
aromas tickling your nasal passage,
scraping at the small hairs there
with a need for spices in mixtures—
cinnamon, saffron, flour dusting
the space between hunger and desire.

They show themselves, unexpectedly,
peeking out just enough to be seen
by those who are looking, listening,
tasting the air like a snake in that grass,
slithering among them, hunting them,
and those of us who hunt, spend a lifetime
learning to read the secret language of ideas.

Second Place, Budd Powell Mahan, Dallas, TX

Out of Ireland
(Rondeau Redouble)

I come from famine, I must bear in mind
the fortune of my birth. My wealth is willed
from kin whose names I know, the hopeful kind,
who came with nothing, hungry and unskilled.

Their emptiness was vast, remained unfilled
in years of brutal servitude and grind
that left the table scant, the spirit chilled.
I come from famine, I must bear in mind

the sacrifice and not be disinclined
to praise the ethic word and deed instilled,
to look into ancestral eye and find
the fortune of my birth. My wealth is willed

from tuber rot and fallow fields untilled
and brothers of the gene who stayed behind.
My freedom, opportunity were spilled
from kin whose names I know, the hopeful kind.

They came with just a dream, completely blind
to magnitude of what it took to build,
to thrive. How could the crude and unrefined
who came with nothing, hungry and unskilled,

become my fathers sated and fulfilled.
With gratitude and tribute intertwined
I lift from heritage a mighty shield,
an appetite for life from blood divined—
I come from famine.

Third Place, Joyce Gregor, Westcliffe, CO

Harlem Renaissance 1957

I trudged up step after step after step.
How many flights fit tight between these walls?

> *I was sixteen and green,*
> *as I recall.*
> *Lulled to sleep by cricket strings*
> *and open space*
> *that came face to face with horizons,*
> *and rainbows end to end.*

Eight flights still!
Energy strangled by a stifling stairwell.
Slow stepping gave me time to think.
Arrange the shoes of others on my feet
while mine left leaking footprints
from the drizzle on the street below
where crushed rainbows
lay in greasy patches
and steam villains swaggered
from the mix of moisture and concrete heat.

> *I remember also,*
> *the style of naiveté*
> *I wore at sixteen—*
> *a yellow slicker—*
> *sanguine, basing my sense of reality*
> *on another place, with open space.*

Leaving street splatter
on worn treads and splintered wood,
scaling the dusty flights, I moved,
reaching, the tenth-floor flat,
a cubical housed with faces
saturated with talk.

There,
in an unfamiliar atmosphere,
I sat
listening to word-drops of hope
patter on a warped floor.

> *Where I came from hope was a routine,*
> *picked up every morning*
> *as I dressed*
> *and shoved in my pocket.*
> *Their conversation*
> *held no meaning for me, at sixteen.*

That was the year
the seed was planted.
Somehow the puddles and gutters
gathered dust from passing feet,
mine too had walked that street.

This gathering of dust became the soil
from which many voices sprouted
in song,
defying summer's heat,
harvesting a Renaissance chorale.

> *Eventually, I took my leave,*
> *on an elevated flight—*
> *a panoramic view of life—*
> *and landed in my space,*
> *wading in a sea of strangers unaware*
> *of an evaporating culture sprouting new hope.*

First Place, M.E. Hope, O'Fallon, IL

Understory

The twelve deer, a dozen dun
apostles, barricade the trail.
A line of slim bodies
as though their legs have become
rooted to earth as trees sway.
Flicking ears match the branches'
motion and their eyes look from us
to the shadow ahead and there
is the thirteenth body, the unlucky
one, head low, one leg slack
and useless.

What can we do here? We listen
as finches sing and cascade through
the cedar, small currents of air
turn to flutter as their forms stream
past. Back up the ridge, wind
is building and comes over the pines:
a crescendo that accompanies needles
and duff, the scent of rain.

The animals turn their heads as the wind
reaches them, tuck their muzzles
toward the earth. Some shiver their backs
as the scatter hits their hides, except
for the injured doe. She continues
to hobble, comes out of the shadow
and walks past each herd member
and as each raises their beautiful face
to her, a purring bleat is heard.
She stumbles down the row, eight,
seven, six until she reaches the last
and slides back into the shaded wood,
back into the brush and cool understory.

The line of twelve turn as though
this moment has been rehearsed over
and over, they follow her
until they all have become tree and shadow
and memory. We turn on the path
back the way we've come, wherever
we'd been headed no longer important.

Second Place, Libby Casey Irwin, Woodbury, MN

Upon Looking at a Photograph I See
What Gifts Children and Stars Are

cherub-chub small arms reach out from loosening fetal folds
plopped on wet white sand a cush toosh the he-human-baby appeals
without words

with baby arms stretching upward toward the sun where is his father's
face who
gazes down, knows his own frailty, that he really is neither God nor sun but
he who

bending over, allows his son to bask like a tortoise in the sun-drawn shade
shadowed summer teaching sea story with his strong, lank arms and limbs

back from swimming now paddling, in his son's eyes, himself, whose sun
and broad eyes necessarily shield

waving off the left-over but precious, ozone he, too, breathing images of
unsaid words but we get the picture

of this sea in the tide of throated airs which spring with a few salt tears
but this new
babe with new-earned sense knows touch-and-hug and slurp-kiss already

with his bending-over-body-dad both laced in and of one's wife,
one's mother in
context behind the digital lens attached. She carries and catches
these moments

extinct time frozen, prophesied and recreated and reprised wet mirrored
sand-shimmer brown sepia mother

whose photo would take over in each flowing and bubbling over of sea
waves milk-edged.

uncovered silt ocean floor water, drenched and lowing, lulling tides who mosey then
dance the boogaloo; swim eyes to the vast up-looking sky and blink eyes star

where the Creator has painted universes like these two generations focused on each
other the symbiotic, the likely tidings this great joy like gramas and toys, shovel, pail

play little lad in shadow cast of your towering-over dad so you can see
down from sky, the slender shadow suspends now, low tide's pleasure to his photo

mother softly makes and takes what she sees and where she suspends
her own brave visage, and vision, also now, the picture is done in 4/4 time

until her dark room doings reach the white of sun stars where are the sun-
reddened icebergs of five seconds worth of dna passings. O God, we are this!

Third Place, Maggie Kennedy, Brookfield, IL

Child's Body Found in Park Lagoon

Pick the blue cornflowers,
the swish and sway of wild primrose.
Pick what is sweet and helps you forget.

I'll sit with you, as long as it takes.
Sing you songs of crimson clover
and ox-eyed daisies until you hear
the dead calling, the little ones playing
hide and seek in the cattails.
I helped them cross as I'll help you.

You know me. I whispered
in your ear whenever the big man yelled,
before the hand struck.

Let me comb out the muck, braid
a crown of dandelions for your curls,
knit you a dress of golden yarrow.
The bad part is over.
Your story just beginning.

I'll rub healing balms of
marigold and chamomile on
your bruises, tell you tales of
sweet William and his black-eyed Susan
so you'll stop thinking about
the steel weight that dragged
you under the water lilies
into the silent fury of tadpoles.

Pick the hummingbirds kissing the poppies,
the white moths drinking their fill.
Pick my hand.

First Place, Robert Schinzel, Highland Village, TX

Flotsam and Jetsam

(In Memoriam Poem)

The ocean waves wash objects in,
    well-worn and weathered by the sprays.
    Their sagas speak of castaways
who foundered where the tide had been.

These dull discarded scraps might tell
    of conflicts unresolved by time
    or unforgiven for a crime,
detritus carried here by spell.

My struggling fingers touch the sands
    to grasp a bobber, faded white.
    Its central shaft which holds line tight
escapes my grip through aging hands.

I wonder how a tiny thing
    transported to this coastline beach
    could take me where but hearts can reach—
a mountain lake in early spring.

I see my father in his boat,
    his arms burnt brown from years of sun,
    the only salt, in tales he spun,
his loneliness the thing of note.

With empty home yet on his mind,
    his feet upon a rotting plank,
    he casts a bobber toward the bank,
unfinished burdens left behind.

My eyes return to churning sea
    to stare at stories in the surf
    where flotsam floats until the turf
claims jetsam as its own debris.

I close this diary by the bay,
    each shard but entry on a page,
    old wreckage cast upon a stage
Too much to read, too much to say . . .

Second Place, Jerri Hardesty, Brierfield, AL

She Was My Hero
(In Memoriam Poem)

We kept our vigil day and night
Those last two weeks before she died,
And through that time, with heart we tried
To find the words and say them right.

She barely seemed to be aware;
The drugs to stop her pain were strong.
We played her music, sang along,
I think she knew that we were there.

She'd been my hero all my life,
Protecting us with all her might,
She lived to share her loving light
As daughter, sister, mother, wife.

On Sunday, as the stars winked on
We closed our eyes to take a nap,
The nurse awoke me with a tap
To tell me that my mom was gone.

I touched her face to say goodbye,
Her perfect skin now white as fleece,
"Goodnight sweet princess, rest in peace."
In state of shock, I couldn't cry.

In hindsight now, I cannot doubt
Her final act of love so deep.
She waited till we fell asleep,
She tucked us in and tiptoed out.

Third Place, Sara Gipson, Scott, AR

Father's Funeral
(In Memoriam Poem)

We climbed the grassy hill once more
    to visit beds where dear now rest
    to add a man that braved each test
that challenged faith, the shield he wore.

Among ancestors, seeds of kin,
    we praised our father's earthly life,
    we sang the hymns of hope and strife
then planted Father's bones and skin.

We buried Father under earth
    beside his daughter lost at five,
    the twin of one that stood alive
with siblings bowed around the berth.

We prayed our father's soul had found
    a better home in heaven's heart
    a paradise of love and art
with goodness filling all around.

We prayed our father see his child
    and other kin he often missed
    when walking fields a harvest kissed,
when fishing streams the sun would gild.

By noon the deeds of death were done,
    his friends departed like the dew
    of early morn, we children flew
with tears our painful grief had sown.

But stars appeared to charm the moon
    before his widow left the hill
    to wonder how she'd ever fill
the empty space a death had hewn.

First Place, Charles Southerland, Viola, AR

The Librarius Wolves Reintroduced Into the Wild

She's in the library, in the romance
section, perusing Harlequins to sate
her longing. And as it happens to be,
I'm seeking history, *a lone wolf,* late
in life. In between the Romans & Greeks,
I smell her Gypsy Water wafting, conditioned
in the air above, flung at me through the vents
from end-aisle to end-aisle. And through
the book-gaps in-between us I see her,
elementary, lost in covers, and hear
a sigh, my hearing keen as sight this close
to speech, to howling. How must Romulus
and Remus have felt suckling the she-wolf?
How much more did she, giving suck
to pale pups? I am akin to them,
progenitor to their kind, flung from the stars,
and as I pass by internal combustion engines,
Italy, junipers and keto diet books,
I never lose sight more than a moment,
but she is conscious of me moving quietly
toward her, gives a side glance when I
stalk through land grants and map books,
pausing to read the signs of her, the yellow
smock frock, capri pants, cropped, mid-calf.
She is Venus, no, Juno, her shoulder-
length auburn hair sheen in the track-light's glare.
Freckles dot her face like a constellation,
her eyes in flux, brown like rich sorghum.
I've seen the Spanish Steps and posers sitting
idly in the Tuscan sun—I've circled
the Colosseum's arches on the run
in winter and finding no one home, I traced
my way back weaving a trail to follow in case
a girl might stumble across it, yet here
I am, an arm's length between us,

the P's & Q's as mindful as my thoughts,
as my pursuit continues. She is more than prey;
an ankle bracelet made of gold holds
sway above her foot bare of sock,
her Thalia Sodi pumps at ease, one crossed
left over right when I approach to
speak to her—as if by chance we meet.
In simple language, more complex than I thought,
I ask her what she likes to read and wait,
and wait, and wait. She smiles and says she likes
romance and nature but the selection here
is mighty thin and nearly bare. She's read
them all, she says. She looks into my eyes
and asks me if I know just what she means.
"Yes I do. Have you ever been to Rome?"

Second Place, Kathy Lohrum Cotton, Anna, IL

Lone Wolf

The snow has stopped now, its woolen blanket
smothering night sounds into silence.

Even the fireplace flames fall to halcyon whispers,
this woodland cabin lulling me to sleep—

until your howl scrapes across my skin,
the eerie pitch, high; the wail long, trailing away

like a train whistle across tumbleweed plains.
I ride it all the way from alone to lonesome.

Though you are not visible through the pine row,
I imagine that old cliché picture: a solitary wolf

in hilltop silhouette against a perigee full moon—
you, the logo for "lone," mascot of our isolated lives.

I fill in your details: heavy, snow-flecked fur,
dark-tipped tail and haunches pressed into a drift,

backbone of a winter-lean gray body angled
straight to the uplifted head, ears flat back.

Your black nose points like the tip of an arrow
toward cloud-shrouded stars, throat shooting

that mournful cry into this vast indigo sky.
But you are not a loner, howling at the moon.

No, you, gray wolf, are calling to your pack,
to a life-mate—your voice intimately known

to each comrade of your close circle.
And tonight your cry also beckons me, saying,

Call home. I hear in your pack's howling reply
that this lonely voice will be answered, too.

Third Place, Wilda Morris, Bolingbrook, IL

Mother Warned Me: A Note to the Wolf

That nanny goat left her little ones,
all four, with instructions not to let you
or your kind in the door. But you
turned your feet white with dough
and wheat, treated your throat with chalk
and called out in your sweetest
voice, *Let me in. I brought fine treats.*
The kids were deceived; the nanny, bereaved.

Now you beg to come in my door.
Lies ooze through your sharp teeth,
your eyes cagey, your growl
more like a bleat as you repeat
how you'll treat me
with respect when in truth
I am the meat you want to eat.

First Place, Charmaine Pappas Donovan, Brainerd, MN

Beseeching the Raven

I call on the Lakota raven, spinner of change,
distill this time my father rides through—
a time when part of his body is not his own.

I call on the raven to sift through the bones
of all that has gone before, carcasses of the past,
sorting truth from real, that which looks exact.

Flying through time and space, dark wings
harbor the starlight hope of black nights,
pollen clings to the underside of velvet feathers.

Swooping and swallowing the invisible,
transitory as the wind that holds them,
ravens make sense of tangled garbage heaps.

Sleeker than crows, shaggy-throated, sooty,
they need only their blue sheen to attract females,
their commanding caw as hoarse-voiced as Dad's.

I call on their confidence: soaring, gliding,
slow-flapping flight, flowing wing-beats—
knife-sharp beaks that filet their prey.

I call on those among the smartest with wings,
they are crafty, keepers of secrets,
stirring from humans their deepest thoughts.

Bring my father back to himself,
sort the snarls of his bleeding brain,
help him straighten his labyrinth of confusion.

Heal what harms my father, Lakota raven,
time-honored among medicine men.
Steal the splinters from his eyes, help him see.

Second Place, Faye Boyette Wise, Benton, AR

A Note From the Ghost of Edgar Allan Poe

They say among the famous ghosts
of Fort Monroe I've been
observed on Bernard Road
at Shakespeare's "witching time
of night." After all I was the most
renowned enlisted man to serve
at Fort Monroe. I recall my room,
that barren stone wall cell.
My table and chair beneath
a small square window that overlooked
the moat, a wooden bunk, mattress thin
as the flag that flew above the bastion.
But how could I write there.
A collection of my work
was published in 1829.
I spent my last Sunday at old Point Comfort
reciting poems on the hotel veranda.
I died in 1849 long before
the house I love to haunt was built.
It is a gracious, spacious house
and I'm told the ghost of me
looks right at home standing
by the fireplace, a tall man
in white puffed-sleeved shirt,
red vest and dark trouser. My hair
is long, my face in shadow. My habit
is to disappear in gray mist
through the window. Researchers of the mystic
say I am photogenic. A snapshot caught
"the mist" of me in a corner of the attic eaves.
My ghost, they say, is most capricious.
A housewife said I shoved her from behind
while she wrapped Christmas gifts upstairs,

I unnerved her when I walked through the bolted doors.
Romanticists say that I return looking
for something I lost. The phenomena-loving me
returns to Ghost Alley hoping to see
a playful apparition who might
recite my haunting poems
from out of a friendly gray mist.

Third Place, Barbara Ford, Poncha Springs, CO

Fugitive Colors

If lost or misplaced, that which is red
is more easily found. Looking in the garage
I see a red motorcycle helmet, screwdrivers
with red handles, metallic shapes in shades
of crimson, fiery orange, and burgundy,
but nowhere do I spy the round corduroy
pillow I like to sit on outside. The overly
cute patch hiding a cigarette burn was
sewn on by my mother, who was not,
by nature, cute. My newly framed picture
of Jackson shows him seated on the red
cushion as if it were his throne.
In a moment of grief did I put it
in his backyard grave and succumb to
misguided sentiment? Now I have lost
my mother, my cat, and the red artifact
that links them in my mind. Rocks and shells
on windowsills, hawk feathers propped
against small shrines, how can I remember
the when, the where, who I was with
and what the day meant? I've not forgotten
the late winter violets I placed on my mother's
breastbone for her ride into the cremation
chamber, or how my dear friend's father
wore my emerald beret when it was his turn
to burn to ash, ninety years having worn out
his. Under my kinswoman Coco's hands
was the Bluebird Prayer I wrote for her
as she too ascended in white smoke
highlighted against an ultramarine sky.
I have not misplaced everything.
Warm breezes and birdsong pull me
into this planting season. I look for
a new way to sit, and a new way
to accept the rainbow reflected
in the spectrum of loss.

First Place, Julianza Shavin, Fountain, CO

Summer, Newborn, Georgia

You set out for work from your town of 300:
yellow blinking light, p.o., gas pump, church.
You drive through your first countryside
with a six-pack of donuts and decaf.

You are three months pregnant
in humidity a vault.
Road kill fries on asphalt—
squirrels, raccoons, the occasional cat.

Cows stand in the pond, water-beheaded.
Everything shimmers.
You like this job, though it is not your real work.
There is so much else you will do.

Decades hence you are a mother twice over,
facing the empty nest.

That blinking light went all night,
to a continuo of crickets.
You recall the country and its kill,
its maimed and broken parts
flapping like wings.

Second Place, Cheryl Van Beek, Wesley Chapel, FL

The Conch Republic

Every night, before sun sinks like a drop of mercury
in an old thermometer, day throws its last embers
at Mallory Square where jugglers toss sunset into flame.
Crowds sip mint-muddled mojitos, gather at water's edge
to watch evening rise in abalone sky—
slippery layers, seaweed green, periwinkle, red tide.

Breezes salt-rimmed as margaritas, Key West speaks
in steel drums, parrots' squawks, ambling rooster crows.
Descendants of Hemingway's cats saunter the streets,
tails upturned like lucky elephant trunks.

Orchid trees spray plum-lipped perfume.
We spiral painted streets, shuttered cottages—
sea-urchin lavender, conch-shell peach.
Blossomed vines wrap porches like presents.
I bite into frozen key lime pie on a stick.
Its bittersweet chocolate shell clings to my lip.

At the old Civil War fort, Martello Tower,
a garden perches over Higgs Beach.
We wind our way around crumbling brick,
landing here and there to drink in its nectar.
Silver hummingbirds, like green-backed, winged sardines,
fishtail in and out of coral honeysuckle.

We spire up a white lighthouse's winding black staircase,
peek out windows—like small holes in seashells drilled by moon snails.
Beyond its palmy, sea-graped shore, jigsaws
of seaweed puzzle green water, pirate lore.

Outraged by border patrol, in 1982,
Key West declared its independence.
It was only for a minute, but their Southern grit
remains coiled in the whorl of time—
sand, wind, ocean in a conch shell.

Third Place, Nancy Cook, St. Paul, MN

Gulf Oysters Are Dying

I marvel at the mystery:
a cave small enough
to fit inside my palm—

timeless
the ebb and surge
of oceans sweeping

through,
rock 'n rolling:
a creation story

I love each Shrove mask,
mouth in a pearly pout,
temptingly creviced

It's what we all crave:
some dark hollow,
hint of iridescence

soft white gellid tongue,
reaching climax
taste of salt and brine—

But now the hosts
are vulnerable
the sacrament is dying:

spillways, fresh-water
flush, have released
caged storms—

torrents of record
snows & century rains,
rush tranquil oyster

beds. I mourn the loss
of transgendered beauty,
its perfect regeneration.

First Place, Shirley Blackwell, Los Lunas, NM

The Life You Save
(Prose Poem)

Yes, Huntsman of the King, in this shadowed forest where I live are solitary bears with injured hearts. I glimpse them rarely, always from afar. I keep to my side of the river, they to theirs, as we abide in mutual accord. They live as bears deserve to live: unbound, free to snuffle berries, swipe at flies, lick oozing hides, and grub in moldy mounds. They let me be. I leave them to their ways to placate hunger, heal their hurts, or die. I do not ask them where they keep their dens, or why they slash the trunks of standing pines. Such matters are between them and the trees, whose forgiving bark so freely weeps its healing sap to soothe the pain. To bring your hunt, your hounds, your chains into these cloistered woods was ill-advised. *My* bears are not for baiting or display. Wounded, they are wary, quick to rise; but, while they sleep, you may yet slip away.

Second Place, Lori Anne Goetz, Germantown, TN

Leaden

(Prose Poem)

We have no winter wonderland, glistening with frost, insulated in thick ice. In deep Southern midwinter brambles and bracken, winter wheat, and six-inch stubble are a patchwork of umber and rich, dark mud, lightened only by paper-light stands of forage, fluttering in the wind, left for the ducks. Clouds compress cold, damp air, saturating earth and sky with shades of gray and threat of merciless rain. Still waters are black with anticipation; ponds ripple silver when kissed by a breeze or when furrowed by ducks and geese on landing. Bobbing waterfowl flash black and white—buffleheads diving. A somber-hued scene, tranquil until the silence is shattered by a sharp crack: a young drake with teal wings tumbles from the sky, and waters suddenly clouded with silt are tinged with blood.

Third Place, Kathy Lohrum Cotton, Anna, IL

Every Scar of Us
(Prose Poem)

In this cheap-rent meeting room, we sit where the view is lawn and landscape too long untended, the acres returning to native roots. Already, thigh-high heavy-headed grasses dance with foxtail and dandelions; bindweed vines up the bark of oak and ash. I follow the feral scene back to my childhood home, abandoned now at the edge of a decrepit white-flight neighborhood. The little house, sided with brick-patterned asphalt, has been repossessed by nature. Old cottonwoods blow their seed-snow where my bedroom stood, sky for roof, memories etched on the last disintegrating walls. Sixty-second Street, once refreshed with tar and gravel each first week of summer, is now a knife-blade slice through abundant green. The patient Midwest prairie waits to reclaim her natural domain, piece by piece, from boarded buildings, broken cities, missile silos, re-routed rivers. It waits to heal every last scar of us.

First Place, Robert E. Blenheim, Daytona Beach, FL

The Night of the Old Iguana

You're run-down and weary, old lizard.
Behind you, sin and rebellion: an unbridled life.
From Starbuck to Hondo you have run whores and robbed banks.
And killin's. More than you can count.
Common mortal laws, not your style.
You have only heard, with rapturous passion,
Whispering dreams of tequila and glory.

But now, a scorpion being eaten by red ants,
You sit here in Agua Verde, on a saggy straw mattress
Holding a nearly-drained bottle of tequila.
An old son-of-a-bitch
Left only to dregs of ground-up dreams
And wishes of being a child again.

In front of you a young woman dries her glistening smooth skin,
Brushes her long black hair like wind caressing the
    fertile prairie grass.
Your sad gaze from grizzled face is met by her soft warm eyes
And a look that could calm the wildest stallion.
For the moment, a Madonna, this whore.

Squinting, you suck down the last few drops of gold from the bottle
    and hold it before you.
As empty as your life.
But as you peer within it, muses begin to whisper.
You have drunk your last bottle. You have had your last woman.
Now it's time for the other.
Time to play your string out to the end.

So you rise wearily, buckling your cartridge belt.
Then, breathing both woman and tequila,
You drop a dozen pesos on the table and stride to the door,
A bedraggled and wizened titan with six-guns, loaded,
And face your comrades.
"Let's go," you say, each word branding the air with hot iron.

It is time for an old lizard to transcend the sunset
For a butterfly morning.

Second Place, Alison Chisholm, Southport, UK

Fairytale

I've read the stories, know the rituals. She'll think
this is a gentle stroll, a walk through springy meadows
listening to birdsong, counting blossoms.
We'll reach the wood before she realizes.

Strange she picked today to reminisce—her memories
of lazy summer picnics are not mine. I recall
the wasps, spilt lemonade, dried and curling sandwiches.
I'll say nothing—let her have this hour.

We're nearly at the straggling pines,
can see the path that darkens where it narrows.
I'll slow my pace a fraction—let her get ahead.
It's worked. She's five steps further off, prattling
about squirrels. Fitting, that this final walk is stilted with trivia.

That's how I knew there was no way forward,
when every conversation revolved around her—
her meals, her worries, how it took such time to choose
her clothes each day—as if it mattered.
When her sentences descended into querulous rambling,
when she forgot how to break an egg or sign a cheque,
I knew there was nothing left for her.

She'll find a bar of chocolate in her bag, a small bottle
of water. I'm not cruel. She's wandered further.
I can only just make out her yellow jacket through the trees.
I step back slowly, eyes fixed on her diminishing form,
don't turn until she's out of sight.

I check the way we came, make sure
she's dropped no breadcrumbs,
unraveled no cardigan
of threads to guide her back.

Bright day beckons. April lightens the air,
lightens my step. I skim across the meadow,
making plans. I'll wait a day or two, ring the police,
feign concern, tell how she left to visit friends,
never arrived. And I'll be free.

Third Place, Joyce Shiver, Crystal River, FL

Autumn Chill

Papa left in autumn
when brittle oak leaves
frolicked on frosty ground
and vees of Canada geese flapped southward,
a dark, honking tapestry
against the pure blue of the sky.

Mama's eyes were as shadowed
as the distant, dusty road
she watched endlessly,
always in vain.

Our once-happy family was changed.
No more Saturday movies,
no more Sunday afternoon ice-cream treats,
no big, laughing
happy-go-lucky Papa.
Our house was as quiet and empty
as a hollow cave.
Shadows deepened in Mama's eyes.

Slow, painful years passed,
a collage of autumns,
painted oak leaves fluttering to rusty deaths,
skeins of geese threading the sky,
wood fires in the cool air.
Papa never came home.

It's autumn again.
I'm twice the age Papa was when he left.
I hear the honking geese,
watch the crisping leaves,
enjoy the ever-changing display
from my happy home.
But, just like every year at this time,
haunting memories return
and the chill autumn wind
creeps icy fingers into my heart.

First Place, Linda R. Payne, Fairfield, OH

I'd Rather Have a Meadow
(Dorsimbra)

I'd rather have a meadow than a lawn,
no grassy carpet, well-maintained, pristine.
From out my window I could gaze upon
an untamed and unbridled wildlife scene.

A manicured lawn,
like a spoiled child,
demands all my time
and attention

So why would I desire to intervene
when nature's rampant artistry is mine
to savor and enjoy? I'll say again:
I'd rather have a meadow than a lawn!

Second Place, V. Kimball Barney, Kaysville, UT

Never-Changing Hills

(Dorsimbra)

All day I love to walk among these pines
and smell the fragrance flowing from the trees.
A carpet underneath holds twigs and vines;
I could lie down and take a nap with ease.

no phone interruptions
no highway noise
perfect peace and quiet
swaddled by the breeze

These mountains haven't changed since I was born,
nor in my father's time, or so he said.
I'll stalk these hills until my body quits;
all day I love to walk among these pines.

Third Place, Wilda Morris, Bolingbrook, IL

What I Wish For
(Dorsimbra)

I'd rather live where roses grow untamed
and milkweed spills its seed on untilled ground,
where by the windows, forest views are framed
for there I know I walk on sacred ground.

Give me woods
or prairie
and tadpoled creeks
to cross.

I'd rove the woods where Jacob's ladder grows
and Dutchman's breeches sway in dappled light
instead of asphalt streets and concrete walks.
I'd rather live where roses grow untamed.

First Place, Karen Kay Bailey, Blanchard, OK

Fantine's Despair

Fantine by Margaret Benardine Hall
oil on canvas 1886

Against the harsh darkness
Of her unforgivable indiscretion,
Fantine stares into our eyes—
Hers now pale and weary,
    As empty of tears
    As the glass bottle is of milk.

She lifts her brows piteously,
While her fingers grip the crude cradle
In desperation—
Directing our attention to the innocent child.
    Like impending death,
    Frayed black rags
    Seem to creep over soft pink covers.

A doll dressed in red
Has been cast upon the lowly floor—
    A figurative gesture
    Reminding us of her passionate,
    Yet deluded love for Félix.

Still,
Fantine's face is lovely—
Her once smiling lips
Turn downward now in hopelessness,
Revealing more than a broken heart
    As she bears her pain
    In the inescapable light
    Of undeniable despair.

Second Place, Patricia Barnes, Wyandotte, MI

Geometry

A Room in New York, 1932
by Edward Hopper

A circle centers our space.
We have gone round and round,
now we are boxed into our neat square,
not a thing out of place but us.

I would show you the door.
Can't you see the door?

Take it,
or the one-note, monotonous
song that has become our life
will dance me to the window ledge
and a release into darkness.

Third Place, Karen Mastracchio, Spring, TX

From *Sorrows of the King* (Matisse)

I see no sorrows in the bold greens and blues,
in the yellow leaves flitting
like cut paper in front of a fan.
Perhaps the cello, center stage,
might squeal out some sad note
for a primitive king whose land is drought-stricken,
whose village shrinks in changing times.

Don't tell the drummer no one dances anymore,
for what is life without a drumbeat?
Still Sechiya lifts her skirt and twirls,
her long foot propelling her heavenward,
her small breasts firm over the thump of her heart dancing,
ever dancing to plucked strings and drummed rhythms.

Whether sorrow or joy, no matter.
The earth is green.
The sky is blue,
and yellow leaves will dance forever.

First Place, Anita Krotz, Salt Lake City, UT

Eden and After

She is happy before the children arrive,
before the unspeakable. She tends
gardens, gathers purple orchids
to frame unblemished cheeks,
cascade through glossy auburn hair,
curling long past a youthful waist.

Birds sing in the fig tree, lilting songs
that flutter through her heart in gentle breezes.
Thornless bushes yield plump berries
that will float in a rich lake of goat's milk,
bobbing and crowding toward his mouth
as he tips the bowl.

She kisses his blue-stained lips
after dinner, after they offer prayers
of gratitude for paradise.

One day he is away at work,
naming animals. She hears a silky voice,
moves closer to better listen.

You could become like God.
She picks a ripe fruit,
takes one succulent bite.
Red juice drips jagged lines,
girdles wrists. Seductively sweet,
she plucks more to take home,
runs to reach the hut before peals
of thunder pelt the hills, bring
sinuous showers that snake the valley.

Each week she kneads fragrant dough
with arthritic hands, carries a loaf
of wheat bread to the angel guarding the gate.

Cries hemorrhage heavy air
as she stumbles away from Eden.
Weeds catch in her toes.

Second Place, Donna Pucciani, Wheaton, IL

Ending It

Ophelia, mad with grief,
is hanging off a branch,
the willow that sways above
the river's roaring current.

Respect her at the end.
Her wide eyes have seen
every side of sorrow. Life
is now on the periphery.

She knows that love
is never coming back,
the smell of a man's skin,
a world of flowers and feasts

inside the castle door.
Prisons can be luxurious
pain contained within walls
and veins. She exhales

before she slips into the water,
having held her breath for so long.
Her hair lies loosely on the tide
for iridescent dragonflies to find.

Their tissued wings alight,
and kindly gnats make the last
small humming in her ears, her face
a petal floating downstream.

Third Place, Charles Salmons, Pickerington, OH

My Father Cursed

when he toiled and tinkered
with family cars and trucks.
His head, arms, torso swallowed
below the front fender, legs
splayed as he cussed the '82 Mustang
with its metric nuts and bolts
and parts assembled in Canada.
His curses commingled with the clang of
wrenches and sockets hitting the garage floor.
Breaking the stubborn silence
of a spark plug that wouldn't budge,
he let fly profane phrases
bluer than his '77 Silverado.
He cursed the drudgery of auto repairs,
greasy fingernails and grimy forearms,
stained denim, blackened rags.
But he relished rewards of money saved.
He boasted of besting his mechanic,
Uncle Ephraim, who lived next door
and swore with aplomb.
Together they cursed their careers,
the slog and grind of shovel to dirt,
hammer to nail. They batted bad language
across the chain-link fence like a shuttlecock,
foul flourishes blazing summer Saturday nights.
And we their sons surrendered
to the seduction of their diction,
marveled and memorized masters' words,
eager to take the court or field
during Monday morning recess
and share what we'd learned,
the real lessons lost on us
until years later when we must
mend our own bruised knuckles,
bend to the will of our bones.

First Place, Donna Pucciani, Wheaton, IL

Pink Squirrel

This morning a squirrel came to me,
hanging face-down from the linden,
meeting me as I stooped in the driveway
to pick up the morning newspaper.

It was a hoar-frosted dawn,
pale and airy as the cocktail
we used to mix as teenagers,
blending strawberry ice cream

with whatever alcohol nested
in our parents' liquor cabinet.
We'd listen to Dylan, plan for college,
talk of Viet Nam and Dr. King

in a late-night haze clouded in
sweet booze and friendship. Today,
seventeen becomes seventy-one
years on a planet of fires, floods, guns

and a squirrel whose lithe body
is a twitching silhouette against
a pink sky. We meet face to face,
catching the blitz of rosy light

reflected in each other's eyes,
both of us turned upside down,
clinging to whatever keeps us whole,
hanging, swaying, staring into day.

Second Place, Patricia Barnes, Wyandotte, MI

Fallingwater

Mill Run, Pennsylvania

Frank Lloyd Wright loved
the diving-board freedom
of a good cantilever.

In the woods of Pennsylvania
where water dances over boulders
and sings the forest's deep song,

we stand mid-air,
as if an eagle has dropped us
into a geometric aerie.

Geometry as a tool of physics,
physics at the heart of architecture,
architecture on the edge of spirituality.

Suspended above the energy of water's rush,
we jut into a woods of sycamore, rhododendron and oak,
breathing the trees and sky into ourselves.

We come close to prayer.

Third Place, Faye Adams, Cherokee Village, AR

A Hole in the Sky

At one's passing,
shocked silence descends.
Only whispers are heard
in the petrified silence
surrounding hateful plans.

Only after the dreaded
ceremonies fade do we hear
how he joked, enjoyed life.

How he loved lemon pie,
took us to Pegg's for Pizza.

How he patched, sanded, painted,
then buffed to a glossy glow
those vehicles now standing
in our driveways
or parked in our garages.

How he willingly breathed
noxious fumes which later
robbed him of breath.

My Pontiac Bonneville,
one of his special rehabs
poised now to roll over
the 100,000 mile mark,
still drives like a dream.

First Place, Budd Powell Mahan, Dallas, TX

One Journey on the Railroad

(Shakespearian Sonnet)

*Robert Brown escaped from Martinsburg, WV
after failing to convince anyone in the area to
purchase his family. He rode to freedom on the
night of December 25, 1856.*
— West Virginia State Archives

His wife and sons were sold five days before
he fled into a stormy freezing night.
He broke the ice that rimmed the river shore,
to ford the cold expanse and ride in flight.
From Martinsburg he rode for forty miles,
then left the horse that had no more to give.
He used his skills, undaunted strength, and wiles
to find the place he dreamed, a place to live
beyond the blind caprice of other's will.
He walked two days to reach the underground
in Harrisburg, where he was kept until
a route to Philadelphia was found.

For Robert Brown the cost to claim his life,
was four young sons and one devoted wife.

Second Place, Charles K. Firmage, Eagle Pass, TX

Listening for Trains

"Seems that everybody's leaving town,"
the words to the song run through
my head as I walk along
the railroad tracks. Mama doesn't
want me playing here, she says
they're too dangerous. But I keep
my ears open for the trains. Long and silver
like the river that flows nearby,
the rails wind west through towns I've
only heard of, as they wind through
my dreams, taking me away.
Charlie Rich's song, "Good Time Charlie's
Got the Blues," tells about folks moving
out to L.A. They're moving, but I'm staying.
The railroad trestle crosses the river like
a bridge to another world, but I seldom cross,
so I sit and watch raggedy men being
chased along the trestle by the sheriff and his boys:
Some get away, others jump
into the river and the rocks below.
"Some gotta win, some gotta lose, Good time
Charlie's got the blues." Summers
I'd play with my friends. When bored,
I'd kick dust at grasshoppers and watch
them fly away with their wings clicking.
Sometimes I'd dangle my feet over
the trestle and see kingfishers waiting
in the willows by the river, waiting for fish
and frogs. More folks moving away since
the cannery closed. Bank and barbershop
are gone, too. Willie, a kid I knew,
got killed by a train, didn't hear it coming.
I watch the town growing smaller,
but Pa keeps on plowing his fields. When
he doesn't need me for chores, I sit
on the trestle, not far from where
Willie bought it, listen for trains, and throw
rocks into the river.

Third Place, Lorrie Wolfe, Windsor, CO

Bipolars and Borderlines

I must set borders, protective
boundaries around my heart-strings.
You are an invader in my new art of
equilibrium.
I startle when the phone rings.

When your name rises up on the screen
I dare not answer.
I know you'll ask me
for help, some impossible task you
want me to do for you.

How can I refuse? You are my child.
But you only call when all others fail you.
You have been too wild to keep
friends, then too idle as
your mood swings from manic to slow.

Then you move in blues so low
I cannot reach you, and
I don't want to preach to you.
So I don't answer the phone
though I know you know I'm home.

First Place, Lisa Baldwin, Grants Pass, OR

Draft Field Guide for the American Girl

We won't lie to you, Girl.
We are here in tricky times,
Treading tricky ground.
Learn to read the lay of the land.
Learn to use a field guide.
Learn. Start by knowing that
There are many good men
And there are many other kinds.
Learn to distinguish sub-species.

Use caution around the loud ones.
Their self-serving noise will over-power
You first, and stealthy intrusions will follow.
    You'll hear these men
    before you see them,
    smell them after they leave.

Don't trust too quickly the eloquent ones.
Their poetry seduces and softens their lies.
They will talk you out of your self.
    You'll feel these men
    before you touch them,
    carry them after they're gone.

Let the wanderers wander,
Let the needy ones need.
Your work is not their keep.

You must care for you and do
What you can to shield
Your true self and soul pursuits
In a culture that would put you down.
Learn the tricks before you take the field.
Learn. Then stand your ground.

Second Place, Clela Reed, Athens, GA

Women's Hands: A Primer

Perfect the solid handshake.
Rub the aching back.
Smooth the sheets from the center out,
to chase the bodies' dents,
patting lumps, fluffing hollows,
leveling the playing field
with long, deliberate strokes.

Hold the crying infant close,
one hand behind her neck
near your humming lips,
one holding tight the bundled bottom
against the comfort of your sway.

Gather the edges and fold to the center
before you lift the cloth to shake outside
the crumbs of daily living.

Pinch the dough along the rim just so
to corrugate the pastry's dam
that stops the tide of bubbling fruit,
sugar burning black as coal.

Touch the men of other women
briefly, if you must, on the shoulder
or the forearm. Never let cool fingers
linger to enjoy a bit of warmth.

Grip the wheel, the reins, the rail. Hold tight
the tray of cups, the toddler's hand, the iron
above the wool, but know when hands must loosen
and release. Give up what is not yours to keep,
pat farewell, wave goodbye.

Third Place, Harvey Stone, Johnson City, TN

Sexual Syntax

Men think in capital letters;
women are conditioned to be lower case, e. e. cummings.
Men get Times New Roman or Arial Black
14-point font or larger;
we deal with Arial narrow,
10 point or smaller and the pretty ones,
perhaps italics.
They think of themselves as Proper Nouns;
we get the adjectives and adverbs
to provide colorful context to their words,
creating mood and tone, art and refinement.
They claim the action verbs, present and future tense,
the imperative with exclamation point;
we may be allowed a shy interrogative,
with a question mark.

But those proper nouns and powerful verbs
forcing adjectives of their choice to
perform adverbs of their choosing
will be grammatically corrected.
The silent e's have found their voice.
"Time's Up" unifies, demanding change:
grammatical equality,
rights to nouns and verbs,
equal font size
and the ownership of No!
For women's role in the language of life
has been long presumed and persistently kept down.

First Place, Crystal Barker, Los Angeles, CA

105 Pounds of Fierce

Wrapped in a cape of feminine, she is a soul of polarities:
Yin and Yang; strong and vulnerable; procurer and donor; kind and firm.
While grounded in science, evidence, and research,
she believes in the Universe Creator;
has unshakable faith of which she feels no need to explain.
Embraces energy and the invisible.
Her shapely frame sports colorful accents that mesmerize while
gracefully moving.
She strides with power from point A to point B in but a jiffy,
for she wants to lose no time so she may experience more.
Her large almond eyes have flecks of golden surrounding the irises
reflecting a pool of compassion with black pupils dilated
to take in the marvelous of the world
that she still beholds in wide-eyed wonder—
crowned with eyelashes curved upwards, long and beautiful;
so strong and pointed they can pierce one's heart.
Raven-black hair frames her face with flowing curls when she allows
all natural,
or at times she wears atop her head accenting the role of she as MD teacher.
She speaks words that are kind, but her tongue can unleash a volley
of thunder
when boundaries are pushed by others who misjudge her tender as
being a fool.
The right of her brilliant mind can pour out creations of her own design
for clothing, gardens or home; or, she can easily switch to left brain
for provision
of a prescription and treatment recipe to return a failing body back
to health.
She has healer hands that she uses to give a pat on the back or
hold the hand of a troubled Veteran. But, she can punch a jugular
without hesitation,
and with expertise guides needles into flesh to inject medications of relief.
Her virtues as a woman are amplified by her protectiveness of friends
and family;

carries the yoke of eldest daughter/sister responsibility upon her shoulders
like a Persian Immortal.
She has enough, but still, fills her days with extra work in a desire to give
to those who have less than she.
She has had lovers and lost lovers, yet she remains alive inside—
holds open a vibrant un-sclerosed heart for the next to find,
having self-cathed and gained an ever deeper understanding
in the equation of intimacy.
While she ponders her purpose in this life she shares her shine with others;
collects followers who love and admire
her beautiful,
her powerful,
her feminine,
105 pounds of fierce.

Second Place, Jerri Hardesty, Brierfield, AL

Wild One

She
Has sarcasm
In her posture,
A constellation of attitude
Orbiting her gravity well.
She is brilliant cut,
Sharp and dazzling,
Always showing a reflection
You didn't see before.
Her eyes can own you,
The curvature of her genius
Has just the proper arc
To be perfectly outrageous,
The bend of her logic
Irresistible in its precision.
She conducts laughter
Like a maestro
Leading an orchestra,
Composes truth
Into symphonies
That seep into the pores,
Melodies that linger in the blood.
She has a pirate soul,
A renegade spirit,
Can keep her balance
On a tilting ship,
Doesn't put up with any slip;
She is her own captain,
A heroic figure
Riding wild waves,
Hands firmly on the wheel.

What Should Have Been in the Obituary

First and foremost, in times of crisis
she was always there with a fresh cup of tea,
brewed the old-fashioned way in a big Brown Betty teapot,
with a blue knitted cozy tucked on it.
Second and next most,
she made the best loaves of banana bread,
moist and buttery, laced with crunchy pecans.
Thirdly and not to be ignored,
she was always willing, whenever you suggested,
to slam shut her computer, step away from her desk,
so you two could hit the Open Mic at Donatello's Grill.
Or she would volunteer to ride the Death Grip Rollercoaster
with you on the third day of the fair when tickets were half-off.
Fourth, noted with a chuckle, you could catch her weeping
when the national anthem was played over the tinny loudspeaker
at her son's soccer match; or watch tears streak down her face
at the first notes of the neighbor daughter's wedding march;
or even at the overture of the local theater musical. Truth be told,
she even choked up over commercials for Hallmark Cards.
Fifth and not lastly, she had a spare bedroom
when you needed a night away after the fight
with your husband. She would show you how to
reconcile over coffee in the morning.
She would welcome you for the snowy weekend
when the power was out. She was ready to add
extra cans of tomato sauce and mushrooms
to her spaghetti bubbling in the pot.
She always pulled out a plate if you came
near dinner, pressed you to stay an hour or two.
That inevitably stretched into five or eight hours;
all filled with good food and nice wines
she discovered at the back of her fridge.
Sixth and never to be forgotten, her voice.

You most want to hear her when things press down too much—
her cheery hello transformed any grey standoffish day into
sun with refreshing breezes. Her laughter stroked you back
into deep inhales of happiness just by being with her.

Let her eulogy go on for hours.

First Place, Joshua Conklin, Amherst, NH

Shovel Song

Winter descends in February fashion:
snow then sleet then ice
then rain.

Upon a crusted driveway
my shovel breaks heavy sheets,
and I find a rhythm:
scrape then lift
then twist then heave
over head-high banks.

An hour in, rain now steady,
I fight the lactic pulse of muscles,
temples trill like struck cymbals,
brain begins to work in staccato,
and in my chest the canon bangs.

The storm breaks and the sun hisses
behind cumulus cadence,
a bright vulture in the sky.
I rest
fearing a cliché requiem.
Breath comes in wispy notes
but slowly steadies.

I grab my instrument for the final phrase,
pitch what's left.

I hang the shovel back on the hook,
heart once again thumping.
Yet, it is not until I drip back inside,
peel off sweat-soaked clothes,
take the tea from my wife,
and catch a familiar note in her eyes,
that the great muscle
skips a beat
again.

Second Place, Patricia Barnes, Wyandotte, MI

Respiration

The humidity was 100%.
How could it not be raining?
I was missing something about percentages.

He said he would always be faithful,
in spite of minor indiscretions.
What did I not know about always?

All men are dogs, he said.
All men. He swore.
No use for me to look elsewhere for better.

Inhale . . . Exhale, was what I was thinking.
Wasn't this supposed to be automatic?

It didn't mean anything to him, he said.
My lungs indicated that it was no trifle to me.

He brought me flowers, candy.
I didn't smile.
Inhale . . . Exhale.

He thought I was holding out for jewelry,
hinted that he thought I was a little greedy,
told the jeweler he felt "put upon."

I was too busy breathing to open the velvet box.
Inhale . . . Exhale took all my concentration.
He slammed the door on his way out.

It started to rain.

Third Place, Susan Chambers, Mankato, MN

Prediction for Tomorrow

The rain has been cello for two days.
I have been gone half a week.
When I return,
I expect only momentary warmth,
a fast fire which flares up too like
a breeze which promises to push damp
away but whimpers into whispers.

I long for an oboe wind
that rolls in slower,
but hangs deeply for days.

I will return. Your welcome will
be one shallow cymbal kiss.
Then you will turn back to the evening news,
because the weather report is coming.

Upstairs, drops will tap a concerto
on my dark window
while I fold away
my songs.

First Place, Kathy Lohrum Cotton, Anna, IL

I Won't Tell You About the Cat

You, who have within your walls
the breath and beating heart
of someone you adore

or long ago agreed to love,
you who set the table
with two plates or more,

who absently touch a hand while
passing the morning paper—
you are not the one I will tell

about these feline comforts:
the sound of little steps
clicking across hardwoods,

the funny flick of a quick
tongue lapping water
from her bowl at night,

warm purring fur
pressed beside me in sleep,
velvet ears that turn

toward my voice
as though every word
is her name.

How could I explain to one
unacquainted with silent walls,
the import

of a small brown cat,
the life-affirming rhythms
of her breath, her beating heart.

Second Place, Martha H. Balph, Millville, UT

To the Manner Born
(Senryu Sequence)

Queen Nefertiti
reigns supreme from her throne
on the windowsill.

I pay obeisance
with offerings of tuna.
She deigns to descend

from throne to floor, then
drapes herself around my legs—
trips me. With a purr.

Third Place, Virginia Mortenson, Des Moines, IA

C Is for Chloe, the Care-Giving Cat

A soft, yet sober tone emanates
from the nursing home tonight.
In her bed frail Mabel Mahoney
blinks at the light, a light brighter
than any star beyond her window.
She feels a flutter, angel wings
against her skin when resident cat,

Chloe, slides in beside her, nestles
under her arm. How soothing to hear
the purr, to sink her fingers into silky
fur. Although doctor, nurse, minister
whisper, Mabel picks up words:
"Instinctively, cats know when end
is near." Mabel closes her eyes, pictures

scenes of her life: writing in a tablet
at her school desk, the tips of her blond
pigtails plunged into Billy's inkwell
behind her; the edges and circles of ice
skating on the pond, warm inside
her wool coat, watching her puffs
of frosty breath; the cold surprise

of her favorite ice cream, butterscotch,
on her tongue; the feel of her fingers touching
piano keys, the lingering lilt of the hymns
she played for Sunday School
at the little white church. Her first kiss—
what was his name? Will, her one
and only love, a love lasting her lifetime;

her students, especially the needy ones
like Wendell, the boy she baked a birthday
cake for, the first he ever had;
and her many kittens and cats,
all beloved from the beginning until now
with Chloe, the cat's image lifting
her; her golden hair aglow.

First Place, Carmel Morse, Lima, OH

Ghost Insomniacs
(Free Verse)

The clock reads 12:48 a.m.
Rudi the dog rests her head
on my ankle, her breathing
comes in tiny snorts
like air through a tin horn,
my eyes are open wide
in a barn-owl stare.
Ghosts are visiting again.

I feel Mom tucking me in bed
under crisply ironed sheets,
safe, secure from dark.
I hear my sister Greta's laughter
like tubular bells
in a March breeze,
smell Auntie Emma
cooking Spanish omelets,
the scent of onions and jalapenos
mingle with her Tabu cologne.

My senses reconstruct
as my brain deconstructs
in the pre-sleep pinnacle of night.
The clock hands drip minutes
in a Salvador Dali daze.
I feel craziness approaching,
climb out of bed, steal
downstairs, grab my journal,
pour a glass of Pinot Noir,
try to put my ghosts to rest,
tuck them between the crisp
pages and straight lines,
sheets pulled tight
under their chins.

Second Place, Susan Campbell, Mansfield, TX

The Pigeons of Paris: The Fire
(Free Verse)

Unlike the tourists dazed by sights and fatigue,
ordinary pigeons, fewer than in other cathedral
plazas, still walk here, coo, peck. Grey and dull
white, iridescent blues and purples, mindless
almost and certainly heedless of the crowd,
ordinary pigeons don't pay much attention,
scattering except when a child rushes them.
This morning the smell is oppressive—
soaked ashes, dank smoke that's brought flakes
of debris. That awful odor after every conflagration.
Four hundred *pompiers* worked all night—the spire
collapsed anyway. A miracle the rose windows have
survived. Snakes of hoses, heaped stone and charred
wood fallen from above, puddles of worse than mud.
And it's raining, the brutal spring cold rain.
Pigeons have been waved off to rooftops
by slow groups of officials who survey, calculate,
investigate. In a land of the non-practicing, they
nevertheless celebrate the three great bells:
baptism, marriage, interment. And midnight mass
at Noël, is watched everywhere in homes, no one
taking elements among the crowd of worshipers.
A world of skeptics bemoans the loss
of this country's *patrimoine*, and believers
weep as this week moves slowly
to a Sunday climax. Where will they worship
now? The pigeons are descendants of all those
that monitored the rise of the cathedral
from the eleventh to the fourteenth centuries
—the masterpiece of human generations: masons,
glaziers, smithies, carpenters, and the women
who clothed and fed them, who probably

never put out crumbs for the pigeons,
who probably had good recipes for squab. More
tourists will come even for these ruins, which
they will recall with selfies: *I was there when …*
They'll be among the financial donors who believe
history, architecture, and art merit no less care
than the planet. There will be more pigeons bred
and hatched here to watch the cleaning up,
the rebuilding. Surely the rebuilding.

Third Place, Diane Glancy, Gainsville, TX

A Long Ride

(Free Verse)

*After his killing in A.D. 661, Imam Ali's followers feared for
the desecration of his corpse. They placed it on the back of
a camel and made the beast canter until it dropped. That
spot would be the burial place.*
—Christopher Hitchens, "Afghanistan's Dangerous Bet"

I took I-15 instead of 80 because I didn't want to cross
Wyoming again with its land and land and land.
Snow fences were the only thing happening there.

At Highway 50, Utah, I took the unknown cut-off south
from Scipio to Salina to connect with Interstate 70.
I wanted to drive the rise and fall of roads
not seeing what was ahead except by faith the roads
were there with lines like veins across the map.

All that way I listened to Christopher Hitchens' essays.
I was hooked on his cool intellect, his righteous indignation.
I read the cover of the 24 CDs
when I was stopped for road repairs—
". . . the principles of reason and tolerance and skepticism . . .
define and inform the foundations of our civilization."

Afghan's dangerous bet was democracy
overriding the old war lords who subjugated their people.

Hours later, I passed the stacked cliffs of eastern Utah.
Always on the backs of others is the history of the world.

Listening to Hitchen's essays, I thought of a brilliant man
who traveled the globe to hotspots to report moral dilemmas
and review and remark on the difficult situations.
It was disease that finally rode him—faster, faster—
until it was over.

Now Colorado—I-70 east and west side by side
through a narrow gorge—and further—
Glenwood Canyon—so narrow, engineers walked
back and forth to find a way for the railroad track,
two lanes east and west, and the Colorado River—
and finally double-decked the westbound lanes
above the eastbound like a dead man on a camel.

First Place, Meredith R. Cook, Blue Earth, MN

Word Song
(Villanelle)

With the uncompromising dark
Snapping at heels, lifelong we run
To fan to flame this tiny spark.

Centuries dwindle to a mark
Illegible from wind and one
With the uncompromising dark.

We are unsilenced. We will arc
Song into void as bow is spun
To fan to flame this tiny spark.

Planet immense, bird-boned as lark,
It batters veins, it burns with sun,
With the uncompromising dark.

Our flesh encircles it like bark
That age will drop ere we've begun
To fan to flame this tiny spark.

Yet womb it well. No edge is stark
Enough to end this. We have done
With the uncompromising dark
To fan to flame this tiny spark.

Second Place, Tony Fusco, West Haven, CT

PTSD

(Villanelle)

Tears and memories to the eyes return,
from a past of which we can no longer look away
The art of war is an easy thing to learn.

Origins on introspection plain to discern,
lessons from Childhood's games and play.
Tears flood as memories to the eyes return,

How those awards and demerits grew more stern
when dreams of wealth and glory led the way.
The art of war is an easy thing to learn,

until the hell of blood fire and metal burn,
until in tunnels and foxholes the sons of mothers pray.
The art of war is an easy thing to learn,

until grotesque mud soups of inner organs churn,
full of limbless and headless bunk mates in the fray,
the art of war is an easy thing to learn.

For days and yesterdays the tortured soul yearns
as all empty echoes through the ages replay.
Tears and memories to the eyes return
knowing the art of war, not so simple to unlearn.

Third Place, John W. Coppock, Tuttle, OK

Remembering the First One Dead
(Villanelle)

October is no season to be born;
though mild one day, the newest leaves descend
along the way the harvesters have worn.

A mildewed gourd, chill-weakened and beak-torn,
spills tender seeds to freeze by winter's end;
October is no season to be born.

In March, the fawn sleeps safe; its spots adorn.
She falters, walks before the time to send
along the way the harvesters have worn.

Deep snow, warmth, January love is sworn,
and child conceived again shall comprehend
October is no season to be born.

Outdoors all summer, parted, we tend corn;
hot, long hours pass; too tired we meet to mend
along the way the harvesters have worn,

and so the rhythm of our kind must mourn
our baby's fever as short days portend
October is no season to be born
along the way the harvesters have worn.

First Place, Janet Watson, Wesley Chapel, FL

We Knew Them As Boys—
A Tribute to Invictus Athletes

For them the war will never end
    Since many trials face them still.
Yet courage is a constant friend
    When heroes test their strength of will.

For all the perils they have known,
    For all the fearsome scenes from Hell
That haunt them when they are alone,
    Oh, we must love our soldiers well.

Their faces marred, their young flesh burned,
    With severed limbs and vision lost,
How seldom they have ever turned
    To question what our freedoms cost.

Those who crawl advance to stand.
    They walk, then run, through all their pain,
And yet reach out to hold the hand
    Of someone else whose wounds remain.

How brave and resolute they are,
    Who train to make the broken whole.
These athletes clear the highest bar,
    For each is captain of his soul.

Second Place, Mark Terry, Orlando, FL

Enduring Freedom

I noticed him, one leg in brace.
His sun-burnt gaze to far-off place.
His soiled coat was camouflage,
a brown and green and beige collage,
the standard-issue "coffee-stain"—Afghanistan campaign.

One fist was clenched, its knuckles white.
Some scattered coins. "It isn't right,"
I heard him say in undertone.
"It isn't right. These things I've known,"
while counting pennies that he had, his fist still ironclad.

I realized it's not enough,
the money by his tattered cuff.
"It isn't right." That settled deep.
McDonald's is a meal that's cheap.
My hand retrieved the only bill remaining in my wallet still.

I walked to where he sat alone,
and in a soft and steady tone,
I squeezed these words. "This is for you,
in gratitude, though more is due,
for what you've done, and have endured, for freedom you ensured."

He struggled slowly to his feet,
an effort fighting off defeat.
Then offered me his unclenched hand,
and mutely said, "You understand,"
impressing something to my palm. I gripped it with some qualm.

And as I left, I looked to see,
just what it was he'd given me—
he'd held so tightly in his grip.
It symbolized their fellowship,
and willingness to join. His unit's cherished Challenge Coin.

They're given to be meaningful, expressing bond of brotherhood,
a gift he gave because for once, a stranger understood.

Third Place, Beth Honeycutt, Denton, TX

One Smoke From a Wheelchair

Rain falls on her arms,
splashes into tattooed patterns
and slips into valleys
drawn between muscles
on engaged forearms
while tiny streams rush
and spill as if down small waterfalls.

She used to hate water.
Now, she lets it cover her tracks
when she rolls down side streets
for a few stops of a personal kind.
She never stays dry, but even one smoke
helps when she feels steam rising
from parts of her body
which no longer exist.

Out from under a plastic poncho,
her hand rests on a cool black frame
as if she controls the turning of a Ferris wheel
from the highest gondola
instead of wheels on sidewalk and asphalt.

First Place, Curt Vevang, Palatine, IL

As the World Trembles

How can this virus cause such a huge scare?
People are frantic, the store shelves are bare.

What's needed right now, since it's getting worse,
is a strong vaccine like this playful verse.

What do we make of Corona's fast pace?
Well whatever you do, don't touch your face.

Call up the office, and take some days off.
Nobody wants you when you start to cough.

The Veep says sorry, but sadly admits,
this land of plenty, is short on test kits.

I think it's Joe's fault, this virus came true.
Biden went viral and that spread the flu.

Wall Street is sinking, the market's a bear.
Is it time to buy? No, I wouldn't dare.

But pundits aren't scared, not even a sigh,
they're quick to advise, buy low and sell high.

If I catch the flu, then after I'm gone,
can I still buy low, from under my lawn?

Senior Citizen's Online Dating Profile

My roots are snow white; my skin has pimples.
Instead of my face, my thighs wear dimples.

My veins now bulge like purple road maps.
I'm always so tired I need to take naps.

My energy's low. My friends are slow, too.
What used to take minutes takes hours to do.

I'm frugal, you know, I go with my friends
to *All You Can Eat* where the food never ends.

And to the buffet, I bring a big purse
and small plastic bags. Please don't be adverse.

My friends will stay home instead of fine dining.
They love to complain. I'm used to their whining.

We go to the movies, matinee only.
Fifteen of us go, so we're never lonely.

My life has been easy without too much pain.
I still have my wits; I think that I'm sane.

I'm blessed to have lived without too much strife.
I'll sum it all up: I have a good life.

Enough about me, if we are a match,
please write back quickly 'cause I'm quite a catch.

Sincerely,
AWealthySeniorWoman@veryhotmail.com

Third Place, Wilda Morris, Bolingbrook, IL

Dust Bunnies

Who taught dust bunnies to hide under my bed?
What makes them think it's a wonderful spot?
They slink into darkness and quietly hide
behind the dropped books and the shoes I forgot.

It's not their intent to cause me great harm—
they just want to gather and have their own fun.
They hide from the broom and the vacuum, and hope
I'll leave for the day and go out for a run.

While they are caved, so to speak, in my room,
their only desire is to be left alone
to do or not do their very own thing.
But I've got a dust mop; their plans are blown.

I gather them up with a vigorous stroke
into the dustpan and then in a flash
without pity for these cute little guys
I tip the dustpan, toss them all in the trash.

I sometimes wonder if I have been cruel
and with no dog or cat, I have some regrets
for the dust bunnies hiding under my bed
were my only companions, my only pets.

First Place, Ann Carolyn Cates, Southaven, MS

Blank Frame

Our mantel here at homestead is a show
of generations leading up to this
minus one piece of puzzle we all miss;
his picture absent yet the blank frame stays;
so how the father looked, we barely know
departing our short lives the final blow.
He simply left without a hug or kiss
yet gave me life and shared his numbered days
without a picture displayed in these shots.
How I acquired his neat and frugal ways
from bygone-era lives that time forgot
of generations leading up to this.
    The missing, glossy photo makes me sad.
    I am the only likeness of my dad.

Second Place, Daniel Liberthson, Cottage Grove, OR

Reading James Wright

Brief blunt words probe hard
or caress with the gentlest touch
like drifting fur torn from animals
as they fight or rip their prey.

He was a large, blockish man,
dead drunk when I saw him read,
the most vulnerable, terrified
human I think I'll ever meet.

He wrote a poem about
the dread of getting naked
beside your Love: exposure
has no mercy on the body's faults.

Ravaged Ohio, once the green
lovely land of the Lenape,
now locked in dirty winter
mourned its death through him.

He was its saddened simulacrum,
a state of helpless bulk yearning
for rescue, buried beyond rescue.
Wrecked land, wrecked life.

Darkness overtook him, invaded,
pressed in from out, out from in—
coal slurry, black smothering—yet
even crushed all ways he sang on.

He sang his poems because
he saw no other living choice,
only dying ones: stay drunk or
take the blesséd cure: oblivion.

Third Place, Pauline Mounsey, Sun City West, AZ

I Hear You

(Villanelle)

Before the twilight air can settle, calm,
I hear the hooing sound of nearby owl.
He's calling from my tree while night is warm

and fragrant with a hint of breeze. No storm
is forecast. I don't need to scowl
before the twilight. Air can settle, calm.

I've seen this owl before. I sense no harm
will come to me. I answer; wait a while.
He's calling from my tree. The night is warm

with just our hoo's for company. A realm
ago, he perched outside my door, white soul
before the twilight. Air did settle, calm

his feathers; friendly eyes. He seemed forlorn
before he flew away. I watched him. Now
he's calling from my tree. The night is warm

before a phone call clambers with alarm.
My brother's died. I lift my head to howl
before the twilight. Air won't settle, calm.
He's calling from my tree while night is warm.

First Place, Donna Pucciani, Wheaton, IL

Survival

It's always darkest
before the dawn
my mother used to say

when she was sober
between binges,
the long months

when at ten
I learned what made her
slur her words.

Our almost-family,
clothed in her darkness,
lurched from day to day,

plodding to school
and work, father not knowing
what to do except

the daily commute.
Her death has freed us
from her love affair

with gin. The hours
between night and dawn
now appear magical,

the soft relief
of breath and air
floating a gradual light,

like angels descending
with transparent wings
among the laced leaves

of trees outside
a window over the desk
where I write, I write.

Second Place, Mary Rudbeck Stanko, London, ON, Canada

The Stringed Instrument of Words

Paper reclines in the manner of zithers,
quiet until it's touched.
It has been wood,
is open in its urge to announce
an opus worthy of ears.
A barely perceptible stream of sound
resides in a pen,
advances like a plectrum.
A hand, like a whisper,
hovers above.

Tone obeys movement.
It emanates from the posture of print,
from the vast interior
of words. Longingly, it plucks a solo
from individual parts
where grace notes combine,
follow silk-stringed reverberations
till they unite in their stateliness.
This scale of effort is complete
when a poem, chromatic
in its breadth, rises
to a surface that sings.

Words will not slumber in rosewood,
nor will they remain mute,
as if unstrung on the exterior of dulcimers.
They are a symphony
emerging from an auditory core
that presides over paper,
that exercises
the human ability
to strum.

Third Place, Betsy M. Hughes, Dayton, OH

Paper Flowers
(Shakespearean Sonnet)

She clutched her souvenir from Chinatown,
the paper pellets in her nervous palms,
debating whether they would float or drown.
Although her hands were trembling with her qualms,
she dropped them into water in a glass.
The tiny paper balls—they swelled and bloomed!
Each one became a pastel floral mass,
its petals delicate but seldom doomed
to sink. In later years the image stayed:
She felt her consciousness mature, expand,
creating poems which blossomed, did not fade.
Exotic mysteries she held in hand!
The child showed boldness on the future's brink;
the poet grew her words to feel and think.

First Place, Janice L. Freytag, Souderton, PA

Currency

The air is heavy with light,
giant globules of sun that hang thickly,
pressing against eyelash, bouncing against tooth.

Shadows are weak tea swallowed up
in the honey of October noon.

Gold is the currency of the day,
and the world swims through a sea of it,
each horizon adding its coinage to the pot.

Second Place, Martha H. Balph, Millville, UT

April

(Tanka)

her daughter's life
ebbing day by day   my friend
tries to stifle tears

children walking home from school
splash in every puddle

Third Place, John W. Coppock, Tuttle, OK

Any Month

At first, the adult female of our kind
knew only she had bled again with counts,
in nights of twenty-eight or -nine between
and taught the male the rhythm for a child.

To figure when migrations, harvests come,
the spacings in celestial shapes and slants
of moon and sun earned names, became our tools
in local words for times to hunt, to plant.

The mensis, menses, numbered in mere days,
fertility and phase gave us the months;
the earth's relation to the sun, the year.
Its tilt lit summer here and winter there.

Your June may not be mine; your fall, my spring;
a tassled corn, a frosted, broken stalk;
short sleeves and snow; the blooms and barren boughs.
For any given month descriptors seem untrue
somewhere about our slowly shifting pole.

Associate no name of month with these:
the flowers, weather, colored leaves, the glow
unless you specify just where you are,
and if you're in a jail or bed like me
the name of any month won't matter much
except the dates of birth and the release.

First Place, Pegi Deitz Shea, Rockville, CT

Charlotte's Egg Sac

Only when the first
raspberries purpled
and I probed the prickers
to reach them, did I see
the pale orb.

A mother spider—
an exhausted curl—
had laid her egg sac
in the elbow
of stem and branch,
wrapped threads around
a leaf above to canopy
her cradle.

My first instinct: *Extinguish!*
Five hundred new spiders
crawling into my home
and laying their own sacs!?
The exponential was exorbitant.

As I clipped the stem,
translucent movement
startled me. Babies
the size of raspberry seeds
were creeping through
a pinhole and poking
spinnerets into first air
the way a toddler
dabs at squash.

I called my children.
Pajama'd, barefoot,
they ahhh'd at the sight.
Then together
we carried the new born
into the woods.

Second Place, Karen Kay Bailey, Blanchard, OK

Quiet Wisdom

(Villanelle)

Ask the animals, and they will tell you
Everything you will ever need to know,
Speak to the earth, and it will teach you too.

Oh, how we hurry with so much to do,
Simply no time to follow a rainbow.
Ask the animals, and they will tell you

Patience is pleasure, turtles know it's true—
See how water lilies open up slow.
Speak to the earth, and it will teach you too,

That beauty is like purple meadow rue,
Or mountain rivers that know where to flow.
Ask the animals, and they will tell you

The birds and bees and butterflies get through
The storms, and live like there's no tomorrow—
Speak to the earth, and it will teach you too.

How does one persevere, and faith renew
When storm clouds gather and the four winds blow?
Ask the animals, and they will tell you,
Speak to the earth, and it will teach you too.

Third Place, Robert E. Blenheim, Daytona Beach, FL

A Tanglewood Tale

Bleeding I came to Tanglewood
to drift across the sweet green fields
a Byzantine pilgrim of overburdened will
treading in the footprints of the gods.
Holding head askew from heavy heart
I throw out my arms to spread my pain
as a vast damask cloak over verdurous hills
to bask in silence under the healing sun.

The blood blossom you planted so deep
sprouts round my heart like the Walkure tree.
Till suddenly as a shattering quake,
Mahler's Second parts the crowd
rolling the trees and lifting the clouds
resurrecting all from the shadows of night.
And in the midst of the throng it hits
hot and red, between my ribs.
But, astonished, I find myself bowing my head
thanking you for this trenchant wound of agony
for spilling my blood on the fields of love
for your gift of pain in leaving me.
Now free from your arms, I'm transformed by art:
that beautiful Lie that leads us to Truth.
A composer in gilding his grief-laden spring
has shown me one's misery makes music sing.

Going on, walking away
down the luminous valley I go,
I am Amfortas with a wound of gold,
a once-and-future king reborn.
While the dying strains of the "Auferstehn"
through the hills unwind
I carry Mahler's lie
and leave yours behind.

Traditional Haiku

First Place, David Bond, Del Rio, TX

Pure science slipped through
a crack in dove-colored clouds
the bombardier said.

Second Place, Brenda Brown Finnegan, Ocean Springs, MS

Sun through Mason jars:
tomatoes, green beans, peppers—
a kaleidoscope.

Third Place, Janice L. Freytag, Souderton, PA

red clay canyon walls
a pebble tumbles downward
echoes spill outward

First Place, Florene Flatt, Lubbock, TX

The Wall

Last spring I stood beside the wall,
Cold black granite with names inscribed thereon.
My fingers traced the many names Rodriquez.
Beloved name, John Jennings can't be found.
Like a little stray, Dad brought him home one day,
Pencil thin with bean-brown skin and haunted eyes.
Dad knew instinctively that he was running.
I just knew that I loved him.

The boy worked hard to prove his worth,
Bagging groceries after school—
up early to deliver "The News."
Soon we applauded wildly as he accepted his diploma.
Table talk revolved around a college choice for him, but
he left us breathless when he said, "I must go to Vietnam."

Gone, small gifts and letters marked each dismal day,
Each day one day nearer when he'd be home to stay,
But one tour done he said, "The war is still not won."
Second tour complete, my soldier boy,
medals on his chest, was home from war.
But haunted eyes and nervous twitch
were gifts not bargained for!
He'd say, "Those who track me are very, very near!"
Yes, he was home, but prisoner of imagined fear.
So running still, he sometimes would call in dead of night.
"Meet me at the truck stop east of town; don't be followed.
They are close and hope to track me down!"

Years later a stranger's voice came on the phone.
I tried to understand when he said,
"Ma'am, he clutched your number in his hand."
Knowing then that they had won!
The enemy inside his head had pulled the trigger of the gun.

I again ran my fingers down the alphabetized review—
Where is the name of beloved casualty I knew!
Dear God! He fought the fight and gave his all,
But his name does not appear upon the Wall!

Jugging on the Amite, LA

I was ten with my family in my aunt's pontoon
boat trolling down the Amite River with pool
noodles we'd cut into foot-longs and tied
to the middle a long white string with a hook
at the end. We knotted the worms to their hooks
and littered the river with them, their bright pinks
and greens glinting in the river-water foam
like pond stones. We waited till the dead of night
to retrieve the noodles from the brush, by then
we'd hope to see them bobbing between
the brambles of the swamp's edge knuckled
with Cypress tree knees. My aunt sat on the ice-chest
full of catfish twisting in the cold slush
with her legs crossed, her sweatered rat terrier
in the crook of her arm while she hollered at me
hanging over the bow of the boat by the belly,
my arms reaching out into the black water
for a run-away noodle, a fish at the other end
no doubt. I loved that chase. My uncle sat
to my left, shushing my aunt with a pair
of pliers in his hands, waiting for me
to present to him a catfish at the end
of the string, tail arched in the air, glinting
in the glow of the flashlight between his teeth
and a black ball of tobacco bulging from the
caves of his cheek. He smelled of river-funk
and ragweed. It's been years since I've seen
that swamp, but I remember how the fried fish tasted.

Third Place, Christian Shute, Cheyenne, WY

Absalom

Sitting in the shade on the porch
Watching great-grandchildren play
The growing season nears its end
With a crispness in the air this day
Their parents on tractors, reaping
On the land I used to sow
I had no machines to help me
But that was so long ago
Even as a child I toiled
Behind Absalom, our faithful mule
I learned more about life with him
Than I did in my days in school
My mother was a young widow
Who refused to give up her land
She, Absalom, and I worked together
Too prideful to ask for a helping hand
Our seasons followed nature's
Prep the soil, plant, reap, plan
The cycle repeating for years
From a boy until I was a man
Each year Absalom grew slower
But his heart was still stout
Producing crops for America
Through locusts, fire, flood and drought
After every hard day of work
I would brush him as if a steed
Rub his long, gray ears
Before setting out his feed
Harvest was our favorite time
Hard work come to fruition
Absalom eating part of the crop
As part of a yearly superstition
The Fall harvest almost completed
Together reaping a final row

The aged Absalom fell to the earth
And into his earth he would go
I married and raised a family
The years pass like a race
Memories of my friend Absalom return
Tears roll down my weathered face

First Place, Lorrie Wolfe, Windsor, CO

When I think about you . . .

I like to think you are upstairs walking
when I hear the floorboards creak in the morning
instead of this old house settling its differences with the wind.

I like to think the clicking I hear
at the end of the hall
is you tapping out a new story

on the keyboard in your office
instead of some jay pecking on the side of the house
hunting insects for his dinner.

I like to think the music I hear faintly
is you picking out a new song
on your old Guild guitar

one you'll sing for me before supper
instead of that teenage kid next door
turning up his radio.

I like to think that silence means you have
gone on some errand to the hardware store
instead of the house feeling empty.

In early dawn, when darkness surrenders to the light,
I like to think that you have never left
or that you are coming back.

Second Place, Pam Tucker, Washington, UT

Every Word Has a Vowel

Sweet mouth bubble,
butter-souled
seed sound,

bright-yolked
center,
U and I

merged,
a monophthong.
Say *Fr(ui)t*

lips rounded
toward a kiss.

S(ui)ts me fine.

Third Place, Eleanor Berry, Lyons, OR

Concave

The copper molds that my mother hung
all over kitchen walls and cupboard doors
were never filled. No batter was ever poured

into their tin-lined hollows. They were never slid full
into the oven to bake. Their shiny, convex
copper bottoms faced always out. The simple still-lifes

of flowers and fruit impressed into their metal
never lent form to honey-sweetened, nutmeg-seasoned
milk and eggs, setting firm in oven heat.

Dangling from plaster or wood, those custard molds
stayed always empty. Their concave spaces
cupped only dark.

First Place, Carolyn Evans Campbell, Evergreen, CO

Eve Steps Out

I watched you leave the Garden of Eden flaunting
a red petticoat and a jaunty blue velvet hat.
You carried a basket of wild grasses and red apples
for which you have a weakness, and a rib,
a sentimental attachment to your creation.

You were fed up, tired of rubbing Adam's back
with eucalyptus oil and bored with his story
how he emerged from the sand,
shook himself like a shaggy dog and hiked
through shadow-sculptured dunes to the Land of Ur.

I overheard you say to a giant sloth,
He has no ambition, slurps mangoes all day.
There must be more excitement outside the garden.
And he's always bragging about
his clever names for animals. Aardvark! Really?

If you had been patient, you would have seen
Adam leave the garden with a stone cutter
to build grand canals, pyramids, cathedrals.
He really loved temples, building and destroying
them over and over.

I followed you into the Fertile Crescent where
you threw your nice hat to the alligators,
learned to boil herbs and bark into healing tea.
You decided to become a goddess for a while,
also a shaman, seer, priestess, temptress,
donning gold crowns, flowers, bones, coiled cobras.

I watched you move through the land, casting off
all glamour and trying a simple life, a herdsman's wife,

a desert woman, friend to the camel or water buffalo,
learning to love the stars and worship the moon.
Now I see you on the plains, the prairie.
It is here I've learned to love you most of all.

I like your straw hat with a band of dried flowers.
Your hair smells like rain, rich soil and clover.
I love your wild rhubarb pie and the scent of clean
wind-blown clothes off the line. I want to sit
with you forever when the sun goes down,
the children in bed, your husband content.
I want to say my prayers with you and sing songs
of gratitude, praising the close of day.

Second Place, Anita Krotz, Salt Lake City, UT

Cavern Where the Heart Should Be

Time here is measured by conflict.
Forty patients each hour—little rest
for harried nurses.

Wounded are sardined into beds.
Stretchers line corridors littered
with stalagmite towers of gore-soaked
dressings, stained splints, and bandages
stuffed in body cavities once
sheltered by muscle. Like ruby beads
on a choker, blood drops string
along hospital floors.

Triage sorts urgency—fourth degree burn
and wired jaw before fractured limb.
Penetrating blast injury before
shrapnel-ripped flesh. Mortally wounded,
caverns for chests, get covered with blankets.
Military chaplains make signs of the cross
over those curled inside themselves
like waves on Normandy shores.

Soldiers' hollow eyes search
for angels in white poplin aprons,
splattered red by day's end.
Gun thunder rolls long and low
past a mortared moon, but injured
see only kindly faces, hear only
caregiver voices. Distance between
pain and comfort shrinks as cool hands
contact fevered foreheads, whisper
words of encouragement. My father
always said, her touch saved his life.

For my mother, shifts end, sleep comes,
a narrow scribble of relief.

Third Place, Steven Leitch, West Jordan, UT

Lineage of Laments

I don't ask, he doesn't share, our stories are the same.
He came back from the jungles of Vietnam,
I from Iraqi sands.

Both have wounds that never heal.
We see the dead die each sleepless night,
and when we do sleep, our dreams end
with the same screams.

The taste of fear, all too familiar.
The smell of death, in every breath inhaled.
The blood on our hands,
never washes clean.

We share a commonality in battle,
a bond that can never be broken.
We live each moment with memories
that cannot be erased.

We are father and son,
linked in a family-tree of tears,
and a heritage of anguish and pain.

First Place, Robert Schinzel, Highland Village, TX

Writing on Rocks

*At El Morro National Monument, New Mexico,
ancestral Puebloans, Spanish explorers and
American travelers carved over 2,000 signa-
tures, dates, messages, poems, and petroglyphs
in the rock cliffs.*

An open diary, etched on smooth rock cliffs
of Zuni sandstone, documents the days
that Pueblo people chiseled petroglyphs,
each carved in surface varnish on the rocks.
Their symbols speak of ancient spirit lore,
before the Magna Carta's promises,
before the printing press of Gutenberg,
before Columbus' ships would change a world.

In sixteen hundred five Oñate's name
was added to *El Morro's* walls, when Spain
explored the savage land in search of gold.
"Pasamos por aqui," the lines confirmed,
man's need to mark graffiti on a stone.
Nieto carved his rhyming poetry,
a testament of valor in the quest
to bring his holy faith to Zuni souls.

The West was wild as humans fought for space.
When passing settlers paused beneath the cliffs,
they slumbered near the shaded water hole,
a place apart from savage trials and war,
from subjugations taking place beyond.
Perhaps this wall epitomizes peace
where travelers rest, despite disparities,
leave greetings lasting for a thousand years.

Second Place, Donna Pucciani, Wheaton, IL

In Defense of Earth

We can no longer turn our pretty heads
from toxic air and water, fires and floods.
The lust for money's blinding us to all
the tragedies around us: fracking quakes;
the water robbed from rivers sold to us
in plastic bottles that will never die;
the beaches disappearing in the sea
as rising water swallows pristine sands;
the desecration of the land for pipes
to carry oil for wars and limousines.
The fish we eat are poisoned, and our meat
requires that the jungle disappear.
The fires in Australia magnify
the flames of California's Paradise.

But, oh, we love our tanks and SUVs
that guzzle gas and eat up fossil fuels.
And thus we perish, failing to take heed
of all the warnings Mother Earth provides.
Unless the younger generation moves
to action that will save our planet home,
recapture sanity and sight, we stand
to lose ourselves and everything we love,
a multitude of species intertwined,
as we are all connected, even those
whose lies deny our imminent demise.

Third Place, Kolette Montague, Centerville, UT

Three White Moons

I dash to Grandma sitting under words—
bold letters reading COLD then WASHED then FRESH.
That has to mean the cherries on this day
of wilting sun. She lets a handful plop
into the silver bucket when she spies
our car pull off from Highway 89.
She waves, then dries her hands on apron, frayed
and thin from all the chores and times it has
been washed. She dabs one corner to her eyes
to help blink sweat away. The same sweat curls
her hair that's gray, and always has been, I
suppose. Obeying Mama's number-one
supreme command repeated every time
we visit her, *Don't ask for anything!*
I hesitate, tongue-tied, wide-eyed and smile
till Grandma opens arms, invites my need
and folds me into ample bosom, strokes
bedraggled bangs with fingers, cool yet firm.
Our talking is a flood of fragments—thoughts
that bubble over and around like waves
of dizzying and dazzling whirlpool.
It's always so, yet none of us believe
it strange—this talking more with hearts and minds
than words. Our conversation ebbs when Mom
says, *Time to go.   Well, that's it then*, Gran smiles,
Just love and leave me here. She chuckles, then
unfolds a magic paper bag from deep
within an apron pocket, reaches in
and offers three white mints that float like moons
on her arthritic hand—those hands that tend
geraniums in coffee cans, or plink
piano melodies, a few old songs,
the upright hums for her each time she plays.

Our parting's always awkward hugs and *Thanks*.
I keep my eye upon her smile as long
as possible. Her form diminishes
still aproned, shrinking into memory.
At last I settle for the long ride home.
I hold one mint, a white moon, on my tongue,
and savor cool after sweet has gone.

First Place, Budd Powell Mahan, Dallas, TX

Estate Sale Biography

For a moment the warm breath
of someone I never knew
swept across my neck.
A bustle of strangers
intent on more than books
fingered the trinkets of a desk,
the treasures of laden tables.
But his presence was sure
in the thousand books
that claimed the space.
Moving among titles
I found spirit
in choices that put spines
in sanctified places,
and I uncovered the rave of curiosity
in a giant dictionary, wings spread
in mid-flight on its stand.
There was a biography
in the library he left,
a story scrawled as surely
as any penned.
I saw him for a moment
in the rustle of thumbed pages,
bookmarks saving
passage for repetition.
And in his alphabetized shelves
I realized the intrusion
of the dozen hands
stirring the order.
I wanted to shush
irreverent conversation,
longed to sit alone with a ghost
in the million words

that lifted him to his life,
that repeated their sustenance
in his speech and thought.
I wanted to hear all the sentences
he used as markers, all the words
that elevated and fed.

Second Place, Laura Mahal, Fort Collins, CO

no one in particular
(Prose Poem)

Miss Adelaide held a book in the same hand as a slender silver shining tube, the cigarette holder a stylish one. She flicked her fingers in annoyed motions. As if a metronome refused to stop. Click, click, click, click. "Stop that!" she shouted at no one in particular, but Eugene heard, and came to her aid. He offered a plate of Lenox China, white with birds, both cardinal and blue, covered in European chocolates. She set down silver, set down Cather, reached for a chocolate and took a bite. Calming quiet descended quickly, library silence, a fragrant scene that eviscerated old age. Beckoning slowly, Adelaide remembered the gardener's assistant was young and growing. "Come, have chocolate, then read to me, *One of Ours* for one hour. I'll ask Cook to make us goose."

After reading a good book

you will be aware
of an absence.

The yew's black fingers
will wag over your body,
the clouds will go

down among
strict roots and rocks.

There will be
hearthstones
fired in sanguine clay.

The air will become
a mill of hooks burning letters.

Note: Inspired by the lines and
titles of Sylvia Plath poems.

First Place, Lisa Baldwin, Grants Pass, OR

Dressing the Boy

It would not be right leaving
To strangers this intimate task:
Washing the world from your face,
Your arms and legs—all arms and legs—
Your string-bean body, white, smooth, still
My perfect boy. Beautiful boy.

Others might tuck you in
A dark, new suit.
But you I know would pick this
Worn-soft t-shirt, green like your eyes.
I lift you up to something like sitting,
Ragdoll loose, and lean
Your too-young body against my aching breast.

Finally calmed, your head nestles on my shoulder
And I am once again
Rocking you in my arms,
Rocking you,
Rocking you to sleep
In the cradle of the Earth.

Second Place, Geraldine G. Felt, Layton, UT

March 17, 1975

A student, on tour with his college choir,
is missing and feared drowned after he
was swept out to sea while wading along
the beach here.
                    —San Francisco Examiner

Folding clothes fresh from the line,
humming some tuneless song
I'd heard my grandmother hum—
I was happy in my domestic box—
planning supper, planning life,
when the door flew open.
There stood my husband,
hair and tie wildly awry,
eyes red rimmed, bulging.

He yelled something—
something too awful to comprehend,
too painful to ignore.
The floor swayed, tipped crazily.
I made him say it again.
I didn't want to hear it but I had to
and he didn't want to repeat
but he had to
to help us face the awful truth,
threshing the agony over and over.

We held each other and sobbed
then pounded our fists against
kitchen walls until they ached, bruised,
but walls grew thicker, dark-veiled
and could not crumble.

Shepherd

you wrapped your arms
around me
told me not to fear
when our children
face their death
you'll be with them . . .
you'll be near

      in pastures no longer green?
      beside the poisoned waters?

my soul is in despair
as your paths of righteous
are no more
the valley's shadow
falls everywhere
my cup is brimmed
with sorrow

      where is the goodness that was to follow?
      where is your mercy
      for our children through these days?

and when they are gone
when only loss is left
to dwell in my home . . .
what then shepherd?

      what child will you protect?
      what child will you bless?

First Place, Nancy Breen, Loveland, OH

Hallowed Ground

Don't cry for me, Molly.
Don't be bitter. It's enough
that I died. Don't haunt
the station looking for soldiers
who fought beside me.
What they know they'll
spare you—how the rifle ball
splattered your letters with my blood,
how my body lay exposed
on the rocks to Pennsylvania
thunderstorms and sun.

I was just spoiled meat
and tatters, Molly. I was but one
in the shallow pit. Rain
washed the soil from jutting bones
that mark the trench where we lie.

I thought I'd lie in the parlor,
my hands folded over the breast
of a clean blue uniform.
The neighbors would bring pies
and cakes, sit up with us
through the long night. Old soldiers
would approach my coffin,
salute me, call me hero
instead of "that rascal Nash boy."

It's all right, Molly. Gather
the flowers, if not for my grave,
then for the others. Remember
Clem Fielding? Marcus Hoyle?
I thought I'd lie among fallen friends

on the hill, not far from my parents
and our firstborn. But don't
fret yourself, dear Molly.
I'm in the ground. When you
pick the flowers, I'll know.

Second Place, Dennis R. Patton, Alexander, AR

Ode to a Season

Look at you!
Slip in under the guise of late fall. Float the clouds
with bloated cheeks that huff dead leave across yards.
But you are winter harsh and cold daring us to come
out in light apparel. And, unaware, we come.

You laugh.
Once nocturnal, now diurnal, you pounce like a cat.
Play us the fools if you will, but hopeful eyes still see
delight. The dead, the dying, the brown from age,
are touched by your forked, vivacious tongue. It licks
and laps the merriment of heart from life to bring bleakness.

You kiss.
The ground, the grass, roadside weeds, and trees grieve
under blankets sheer and white. You fold out silent snow
in the night like a parent tucking in a child. All objects
once distinct are bumps and lumps and humps unformed.
You become the magician whose hand can cover the sun
and cloud the blue with grey and sage and shades of ocher.

You bring beauty.
The snow banks against the evergreens to ensconce them
making rustic pictures. Holly berries are delicate red lips
and glisten on front-door wreaths. Cardinals and jays
brighten front yards as they invade and search for peace offerings
in seed feeders. Such beauty makes you fail in bringing the ill
your impish smile infers—a wishing well gone dry.

You march off in a huff.
Bring in new winds to melt the ice to mess. Drag your nasty
underbelly of muck and mush and sulk to your corner.
Melt our ski paths and sink our forts. The kid in us regrets the loss.
We've made it sport to play and now you've run away.

Our chimneys wave goodbye.

Third Place, Dave Harvey, Talent, OR

West of Juntura, Oregon, I Hear a Late-Night Truck
(161st day of a long bicycle tour)

> *Gears keep changin' as they climb that hill . . .*
> —Tom Paxton, "Oklahoma Lullaby"

Sleeping in the Oregon desert, here off U.S. 20,
I'm little bothered by late-night traffic;
it's a long, lonesome highway,
and hours between cars are flannel silent.
Once, though, a westbound big rig rumbles past,
       motor roaring.
Just west of me he hits the grade
I will climb, first thing tomorrow.
The engine slows; driver double-clutches—
short snort, as a sleeper turns over between dreams—
shifts down, tries whether the new gear's low enough.
No—motor's pitch glissandos down again,
and again he double-clutches, shifts, tries again—still
not low enough.
Again he shifts down, and again, until finally
he finds the ratio that can match that hill.
The engine steadies on a pitch that holds until he tops out.
There he shifts higher again, drones away,
and in a minute the dieselsnore
fades to nothing in the goosedown silence.

His duel with the Oregon grade brings back
fifty hills as I crossed Iowa, two months ago:
I'd hit each one moving fast, in a tall gear,
riding on momentum from storming down the last hill.
As gravity gripped me, I'd shift down, shift down,
get into lower and lower gears, until I hit a gear
I could keep pulling in, climbing at a walker's pace,
and ride the final yards to the summit,
where I'd shift up and begin another swoop.

Many times a day, as I crossed Iowa,
I tamed each tooth of the saw—and now,
many miles closer to home and the end of this Tour,
I smile to hear that trucker
      shifting down,
           shifting down.

First Place, Jenna Pashley, Richmond, TX

Fountain of Youth

Even if they don't come
looking for a fountain of youth,
everyone seeks the sunshine.

Retirees or families, spangled with sequins,
draped in prints of dubious quality,
they come south to explore caverns,

tourist traps, unaware they're on the hunt
for a single taste of those stagnant,
everlasting waters.

One sip of that magic draught
transports to a past time: of lemonade
on front porches, morning swims with manatees.

Where the grass is cut every Saturday,
bare toes squelch in boggy patches, and
no one itches of poison ivy.

A place where mosquitoes savor
the unrelenting humidity, thick as blood.
Where strangler figs and bromeliads

hang above, between earth and air,
everything in a great sticky state of life,
and the visitors, feeling younger already,

watch rockets blast off, as
ice pops drip red, white, and blue
down sunburnt arms.

Second Place, Cheryl Van Beek, Wesley Chapel, FL

Tracing Orange Blossoms

In Florida when I was small
I imitated puffs of orange-beaked, yellow chicks
following their mother in straight lines
chirping, "free-off, free-off." I traced my days
around honey-scented white stars
of Meyer lemon blossoms. Bumpy-shelled blue crabs
dragged flip flops across the grass into the canal
behind our yard. I wore orange-blossom
perfume sold on a scallop shell.

Back then, transportation was scarce.
Mom and I walked long distances to bus stops
in the stubborn sun till a luncheonette
lured us in, promising just-squeezed lemon-limeade.
When its tart sweetness soaked our parched throats
we revived like wilted flowers in soft rain—
only to watch the bus go by
and have to wait all over again.

After many years away, I retraced my footsteps.
Like orange blossom on a scallop shell,
a tide of salty-sweet memories pulled me back.
Though the lemon-limeade
doesn't taste quite the same,
I'm smiling here again. Planting,
I sift through the dirt looking for traces
of ancient Florida: a Timucuan spear point,
or shards of Tocobaga pottery
below the developers' fill.

Fire ants sting through our yard, bees buzz my ears
dive bombing blue porterweed, competing

with orange and black Gulf fritillaries
for what must be the last drop of nectar.
At dusk, hummingbird moths thwack-buzz our porch screen—
drunk from over-nectaring at the Pentas.
Night-blooming jasmine perfumes the dark.
Alligators grunt in search of company.

Third Place, Barbara Blanks, Garland, TX

The Ringmaster
(Roundel)

The Ringmaster was the star of the circus—
a colorful host, announcer, and broadcaster
of thrills and chills, a champion of hyperbole—*plus*
The Ringmaster,

in his role as upcoming three-ring-acts forecaster,
sang out their praises in stupendous stylistic chorus.
The Ringmaster

delivered a magical world using no hocus-pocus.
He was a consummate audience flabbergaster.
Who was the one circus showman who deserved his own opus?
The Ringmaster.

Note: In May, 2017, Ringling Brothers Circus closed after 146 years.
Their winter quarters were in various cities in Florida, including
Ellenton, Tampa, Sarasota, and Venice.

Dark Cherries

As a kid, she liked sour things: gooseberries stolen
from her old neighbor's bushes and eaten by
handfuls as she tried not to pucker; hard shriveled
dried apricots that an uncle sent from California
every Christmas, that she gorged on until spring;
lemons, that were probably worse for her teeth than
candy, but later, in her first pregnancy, kept nausea
at bay. She got plenty of tart pie cherries from
her one tree, but really preferred them raw.

Over the years she began to prefer milder fruit: Italian
prune plums, sackfuls shared by a generous friend;
ripe strawberries, big fat peaches, and huge blueberries
from u-pick farms in the valley; over-ripe blackberries
for making pancake syrup and even a tangy sweet wine
made accidentally from berries left too long in a cooler.
Apples were iffy, especially the boring store-bought,
so-called Delicious, but she felt a special nature-girl-Eve
delight when she bit into the unknown crackling-crisp,
juicy-tart, almost-ripe yellow ones picked at whim from
the old tree with limbs broken by a scavenging bear.

Sweet cherries were a late preference that seemed almost
decadent. Each year, it was a race to pick Bing cherries from
failing misshapen trees before deer or blue-jays got to them.
Eventually they had to be cut down. After that, she gorged
on sweet Hood River Valley cherries in late summer, and
imported South American cherries in the winter. Finally,
as an old woman in a townhouse with no garden, she
discovered canned dark cherries, always available, expensive
but worth it, soft and sweet, floating in an irresistible
wine-dark sea of nectar she sipped like an elixir of youth.

Second Place, Jonathan Bennett, Lakeland, TN

Quotient

Depending on the integers involved,
sometimes something remains but it
is never wholly what it was before,
and the answer, so elegant, has this remnant,
a hanger-on, no matter the dividend;
and parsing it out leaves us only a fraction—
no matter how rational it may be—
of what we had before the divider showed up
to proof just how many parts
used to make up the whole.

Third Place, Michael Spears, Plain City, UT

The "Black Hole"

They were five dumb boys who never shared
the slightest hint of dare, nor sense of false bravado;
for it was never about: "just because it was there."
Had to be much more than that—
A white whale in the rough green sea
defined their summer of nineteen fifty-seven;
a shadowy hole through a wall of earth,
with two straight rails running imperceptively deep.
They knew it could never be subdued,
nor could they ever conquer the dark, black thing—
But it had to be seen, close up and personal;
they had to know for themselves their fear was real.
Rumor was the other end met the eastern shore
of the Willamette River four miles below
the Columbia confluence.
Five dumb boys on three second-hand bikes
rode up North Woolsey Avenue, past Columbia Park,
crossed the projecting peninsula, and found
the mouth of the western end—
One and a half miles through the earth, it ran.
They measured the narrowness of tunneled width;
lost an entire week studying traffic in and out of it;
calculated the degree of danger, as only young boys can.
Two days later five dumb boys with one Eveready
Black and Yellow Super Lantern, two canteens,
three Hostess Cupcakes and two Twinkies—
in one Archimedean moment made a mad dash
through the creosote-infused "black hole."
Five dumb boys on an anticlimactic mission:
To harpoon that coal-black, smoking behemoth—
But therein lay the surest sorrow of lessons
learned from hallow-rimmed energy spent,
as forty minutes later five dumb boys
came out the other end,
threw rocks in the Willamette River—
And walked back home again.

First Place, Dave Harvey, Talent, OR

Sonnet to an Armadillo in My Campsite—Lake Valentine, LA
(Shakespearean/Elizabethan Sonnet)

Shall I compare thee to an armored pup?
Thou art as bouncy and as curious.
Thou seekest anthills from which thou may'st sup,
Thy nose a-sniffing with vibrations furious.
This campsite was a lone and lonely place
Ere thou, in clicky armor, happened by.
One look at thy sharp seeking ferret face,
And solitude no longer seem'd so nigh.
For thy eternal pup-time shall not fade,
Nor grow less bouncy in this poet's mind:
In there thy rompings through this shadow'd glade
Shall linger, though my face grow old and lined.
So long as bikes can roll and we ride free,
So long lives this—and this gives life to thee.

Second Place, Fay Guinn, Jonesboro, AR

On Writing Poetry

(Shakespearean Sonnet)

If I, by clever words, can make you smile,
a jerk of lip, a silent smirk or two,
forget reality for just awhile,
transported from life's arduous milieu,
If I can bring a magic beam of light
into a world of tragedy and gloom,
dislodge a brick from walkway in the night,
delay the dirges of approaching doom,
If I can charm, beguile, amuse, bewitch,
a corner of a sullen mouth up-turn,
relieve the stressful circumstances which
debilitate and bore, in chaos churn,
If fantasy flicked from my pen brings fun,
well, then, my friend, my work on earth is done.

Third Place, Robert Schinzel, Highland Village, TX

Autumn Chill

(Shakespearean Sonnet)

The unexpected autumn winds conspire
with mountain chill to alter aspen's leaves,
each trembling yellow sequin set afire
displaying faintest blushes in the weaves.
Invasive gusts of uninvited air
disturb the dangling twigs within their reach,
the same way hidden accusations fare
when slipped into a lover's casual speech.
The subtle undercurrents tear and twist,
each breath a blow to one who cannot cope
with innuendos striking like a fist,
a blast of ice, when summer promised hope.
    I thought the bonds were strong enough to hold,
    but now I see this fall brings cutting cold.

First Place, Budd Powell Mahan, Dallas, TX

At Masada

Israeli students cluster for my camera,
smiling in the ruins of ancient lives,
and just beyond them the angle turns vertical,
the Dead Sea lying so far below
that we seem to view it from a cloud.
On this flat top of thrusting mountain
I imagine the world as it was,
the blessing of living on a pedestal.
In these Spartan spaces they lived
as we now live,
not in the luxury of our comfort,
but in the embrace of child,
the cherish of parent,
the joy that bound them to each other.
But there are always enemies,
invaders whose greed steals the names
from faces.
Here in the eye of inescapable onslaught
they made the choice of death,
plunging down the slopeless face
of stone.

I have come to listen for the voice
of forgiving,
to learn the words
that do not speak judgment.
And I find
all the understanding that I need,
in innocent faces and ancient blood,
knowing that
after every ruin
good will always
remain.

Second Place, Betty Kossick, Apopka, FL

Kentucky Girl

(for Susan)

I didn't plan on adopting
A child of Kentucky who
Spoke with an accent song
But she came to me like
The warmth of spring,
And she brought words along;
She wrote gripping thoughts
Of Appalachian heritage;
Her own real-life stories
That taught me of her kin,
Herself, and the hard times:
The raging floods, and worries.
Sometimes her blue eyes
Filled with tears as she wrote
Of her mother, to whom she
Promised to one day become a
Published writer, to make her
Mama proud; so she came to me,
And I mentored the budding
Writer and watched her smile
Grow wide with her accepted
Work—even though her mother
Now passed and does not read her
Child's words so choicely scripted.

. . .

Thus, I adopted this gifted child,
Though woman, indeed, much
Like a flower attracting birds
To her—and I'm Mom-me, the
One to clap for her as a Mother,
Mighty proud of well-spun words.

Third Place, Emory D. Jones, Iuka, MS

The Patriot

Clayton Beauchamp turned seventy today,
But still wears beret,
And cammies,
With tropical lightning patch,
On special occasions—

Like Veterans Day
And Memorial Day
When tears flow easy now
Even when the high-school band
Plays the National Anthem
At football games
With his right hand
Over his heart
And Old Glory swimming
In his eyes.

Half a life ago,
He took names
In the Nam
Amid splash of AK rounds
And RPG blossoms.

He still takes names—
Rubbings
From polished black stone.

Clayton Beauchamp turned seventy today,
But he still remembers.

First Place, Joyce Shiver, Crystal River, FL

The Hometown Oak
(Minute Poem)

I'm tired and weary, almost broke,
but there's the oak!
I've been away;
I had to stay
in combat in a treeless land
of burning sand,
just memories
of home and trees
and hometown pictures in my pack.
But now I'm back;
the big oak tree
spells home to me.

Sprouts

(Minute Poem)

He planted each small apple tree
where youth could see
the bursting shoots
of one's pursuits.

The tender buds of early growth
gave promise both
of winter's flight
and spring's delight.

He nurtured zeal with ceaseless care
to see fruit bear
as children grew
enlightened too.

Third Place, Patricia Barnes, Wyandotte, MI

Everbeauty
(Minute Poem)

An evergreen is neat all year
I never fear
that it will shed
leaves dry and dead.

But maples are a major mess—
worth it, I guess
for displays
on Autumn days.

Yet evergreens, frosted with snow
at ten below,
call Winter's bluff.
Their beauty's tough.

First Place, Virginia Mortenson, Des Moines, IA

The Disseminator of a Sad Truth

Our first-grader's teacher complains,
"Too focused on drawing elaborate pictures."
His pages crowded, animated characters, alive,
dangling in daring exploits. As parents
we hesitate to respond while his brother,
a year older, corners him, feeds him the lesson
he's already digested: "From now on color
a strip of blue at the top of the page, a green
one at the bottom. Stick a house or a tulip
in the middle. That will satisfy her and you
can go on to more important stuff—worksheets."

Second Place, Brenda Brown Finnegan, Ocean Springs, MS

I Wish I'd Had a Black Friend

I wish I'd had a black friend when I was very young,
but I lived in Mississippi; that just wasn't done.
The mystery of why they sat above us at the show
in the balcony, by another door, would be solved, I know.
And why did a neighbor have a separate plate and fork
for her gardener? Was she afraid she'd catch something dark?
Our neighborhoods were distant; so white, remote and clean,
yet Daddy said that Leroy's house was fragrant and pristine
when he went to help him repair his damaged roof,
and ate the cake his wife served, and said that it was proof
that blacks and whites were more alike than most of us could see.
I wish I'd had a black friend who wished that she had me.

Third Place, Linda Treat, Blue Springs, MS

The Broken Heel

I feel incomplete
Without you,
Like a shoe
With a broken heel,
Limping along,
Getting there slowly,
With blisters . . .
But getting there.

How I wish
I didn't need you.

First Place, Jerri Hardesty, Brierfield, AL

Faithful

(Shakespearean Sonnet)

The stars all dance around the shining moon
In patterns preordained since dawn of time,
Invisible in harshest light of noon,
But night reveals their reason and their rhyme.

They twinkle and they wink their sparkling eyes,
All hopelessly romantic little flirts,
With lively steps that tempt the very skies
To peek beneath their bright corona skirts.

Politely, moon applauds for one and all,
Appreciative, but uncommitted still,
Dependable white orb that heeds the call
Of gravity and earthly sky to fill.

Just like the metaphoric ball and chain,
The moon to Earth in marriage must remain.

Second Place, Barbara Blanks, Garland, TX

Hamlet Grieves for Yorick
(Shakespearean Sonnet)

Alas, poor Yorick—I did love him well.
This fellow from my misspent youth who used
to laugh and sing, played pranks—a nonpareil
where humor was concerned—kept me amused.
I broke my leg once—willingly upon
his back he carried me to swimming hole,
to school, to church, to town, to hither, yon—
and, for a laugh, donned donkey ears—his role
he said as beast of burden … harbinger
of future job as jester of the court.
He played with ironies as messenger
of life and death, and made them merry sport.
   His lips I kissed—Oh! Everything we shared!
   But now he's gone, and I am much despaired.

Third Place, Kathy Lohrum Cotton, Anna, IL

Spring Rain

(Shakespearean Sonnet)

Umbrella closed, I walk where April rain
perfumes the air with scent of dampened earth
and arcs her pastel rainbow once again
with colors signaling a season's birth.
The woodlands, softened with first signs of green
in auras cast around awakened trees,
lift darkened limbs with buds still barely seen
and stir with birdsong in the warming breeze.
I splash through puddles, let the water seep
into the edges of my walking shoes,
as skies rouse from the drowse of cloudy sleep,
and heavy grays give way to sunny blues.
No gloomy winter in my heart remains,
for I have felt the joy of April rains.

First Place, Linda Banks, Mesquite, TX

A Secret Distance Keeps

(Hotel Chequamegon, Lake Superior)

Two ladies stroll along a cobbled shore.
Ruffled parasols, like Queen Anne's Lace,
bloom above their heads. They lift their
long white-linen skirts above the damp,
revealing buttoned-up, high-heeled shoes,
precarious footwear for such a place.

They are joyous in their daring on a day
so bright it blinds the eyes. One turns
and smiles in answer to the other's words,
a secret distance keeps.

Behind them, boats skim sparkling waters.
On the hill above the beach, a hotel rises
like a full-masted schooner, white clapboards
gleaming against brilliant blue sky.

Inside the hotel's lobby, Oriental rugs
and antique settees invoke the past,
as does the painting on the wall, in which
two ladies stroll along a cobbled shore.

Second Place, Elaine Person, Orlando, FL

Gala

At seven
years old,
her mother
sent her to ballet
lessons to gain
poise for boys,
to become a mother and a
housewife at twenty-one, to
entertain her husband's bosses
at dinner parties, to cook, to look
just right every night. She was led
by her mother, not by her head. At
thirty, the gala showed her off with
all the celebrities and ballerinas that
she did not become. Dancing class was
a hoax, a ploy, a mask, a disguise for who
she really was/is/will be. No poise, just poison.
No confidence, no confidants. Standing with feet in
first position, she rubs her trembling hands against the
front of her gown as her husband walks by and whispers in her ear,
"Watch your posture."

Note: "Gala," a concrete poem, is shaped as a "woman's back and her
beautiful gown," inspired by the painting, *Belle of the Ball*, by Vasu Tolia.

Third Place, Donna Pucciani, Wheaton, IL

Misty Morning

Alfred Sisley, 1871, Musee D'Orsay, Paris

The fog should have lifted
as the sun rose. Instead it clings
to trees, flowers, un-mown grasses,
and a wire fence like a specter of bones.

The leftover moon refuses to leave,
painting everything the silver-green
of old copper, even the bent back
of an old peasant gathering whatever
she can find, her white headscarf
catching the light of clustered flowers.

Today's mist is not coddled comfort
but raw chill. Even the angels hover unseen
on droplets holding the sum of today's human tears.
Mist is like the past, tainted by time, awash
in fear or joy or the ghosts of waking dreams.
Mist shrouds the moment in a lover's eyes
when love recedes.

The truth of fragility and failure
is its dun color, the glow of gold
reaching for the blue of sky, meeting terrain
that sinks under the weight of dulled aqua.
Mist is wordless, the irrational life
of all creatures caught in its lingering grasp.
One cannot pray oneself out of it, nor medicate
to arrest the soft plague descending.

What used to be pinks, blues and yellows
now melt into each other, a starless gray,
the brush of memory, a bank of moist blossom,
the blur of an old woman's rheumy eyes,
heavy with incipient rain.

First Place, Budd Powell Mahan, Dallas, TX

The Flight of Sparrows
(Shakespearean Sonnet)

The need for *more* is marked in hard cement
that lavas out across the grassland's face,
as sparrows seek their nest and seed, lament
the altered habitat, the quickened pace
at which the black and rich becomes a stone.
They see the nourish of the wild field's weed,
and rise in whispers from the meadow's bone
to satisfy the gravity of need.
Too few are left who saw the green, the smoke
of wings that swept above the waving blade,
and watched the sated flight in which they broke
the pull of earth to soar in summer's jade.

Each day man crowds the native species' space,
and sets the stage to end the human race.

Second Place, Meredith R. Cook, Blue Earth, MN

Fallout

Milkweed
drew in Monarch
butterflies whose wings flapped
as orange and black as Halloween
perennially through my childhood falls,
but have dwindled to rare now
that herbicide is sprayed
on roadside ditch
milkweed.

Third Place, Von S. Bourland, Happy, TX

Blinking Lights Paint Darkness Scarlet
(Pantoum)

Red sky at night, sailor's delight. —Dictum

Night skies light up and cast a festive glow
like sunset on wheat fields or neck-high corn
where wind machines revolve, though seeming slow
to snatch the power found to be airborne.

Red suns blink on wheat fields or neck-high corn
each plodding behemoth like giant bees
who snatch their pollen, then become airborne
but often stop, as if in sculptured frieze.

Those plodding behemoths, like giant bees
who reap electrons from the twirling air
but often stop, as if in sculptured frieze,
grace prairies, mesa tops. They're everywhere!

They reap electrons from the twirling air
above the tumble weeds and blowing dust;
grace prairies, mesa tops. They're everywhere
you look on western plains. Their wings adjust.

In twenty-first millennium, we must
let wind machines revolve (though they seem slow)
to harvest power we can always trust.
Night skies light up and cast a festive glow.

First Place, Julianza Shavin, Fountain, CO

Changeling

Today the mouth is a white box, fisting its fury
though the problem in not mouth but brain,
the black box, and all other boxes:
prism of insides roiling:
this one anxious, that one afraid,
others in ribbons of regret.
It is such a day.

It is not up to the boxes,
not up to depth perception,
all those equilateral triangles
that tell us where we are, that we are,
but depth itself that fuels the white box
with its confounding
it will last, will not last, worry less, worry more.

I want to crush the boxes,
but what is the *I* that crushes,
if not another box, the God I fashioned
from stars and sadness, hope and demise,
flattened corners of an earth to die for, live for?

I watch the sky on these sickest of days
as though only by watchers can a sky maintain,
one lid open as in ease of death
pupil fixed for the next fight,
if lachrymose that heaven seems to salute,
even boxed as it is, by universe, galaxy

until finally rest comes, slow but gathering,
like those little deaths, but innocent,
pitpatting toddlers dragging their sleepers
through and through and through the rooms,
promising release from pain, sphere of warmth,
like love is a sphere is a sphere is a sphere

and finally lips close on the circumscribed day,
now colorless, shapeless, sweet—
sweet changeling, amortal dove.

Second Place, Lisa Baldwin, Grants Pass, OR

Where We Stand

for Dad in his centennial year

I think of you always as standing
on the far shore of Babyfoot Lake,
where the treeline and shoreline were once
one and the same, evergreen and light

before the big fires—
Silver, Biscuit, Chetco, Klondike—
burned through and through again,
burned hot and hotter still

the forest stands still, bearing charred witness
with two hillsides of black and ashy skeletons,
a cemetery of silhouetted crosses
haunting the lake with these reflected ghosts

yet I recall you standing just there—
the heel of the lake between us—
the water both reflecting the light
and swallowing it whole

into the deep, it disappears, only glinting
a little in the shallows of the lapping shore.
What craft might close the span between us
or this memory of trees and light?

Third Place, John W. Coppock, Tuttle, OK

Presenting the Four Seasons As Composed

```
r  w  a      l  u  a      w  p  t      b  S  l
e  h  n         n  w      h  e  h      u  p
a  i  d      r  l  a      i  r  e      d  r  h
d  l         e  i  y      l  c         s, i  u
   e  b      v  k         e  h  m         n  n
t     i      e  e  f         e  i      p  g, g
h  l  r      r     r      t  d, d      l
e  e  d      s  t  o      h     d      u  S  f
   f  s      e  r  m      o  w  l      m  u  o
C  t         d  u         s  a  e      s, m  u
h     t         e  c      e  t            m  r
i  f  a      p     h            f      l  e
n  r  l      l  w  a      l  c  o      e  r, p
e  o  k      a  r  t      o  h  u      a     a
s  m         c  e  t      o  i  r      v  F  n
e     t      e  n  e      k  n         e  a  e
   s  h      m  s  r         g  w      s, l  l
w  p  e      e            o     r         l, s:
a  r         n  o         u  a  e      b
y. i  y      t, f         t  l  n      r  a
   n  e                   w  l  s      a  n
   g  a         a         a            n  d
      r                   r  t         c
   l            g         d, h         h  W
   i            r            e         e  i
   m            o                      s— n
   b            u            o            t
   s            p.           t            e
                             h            r—
   w                         e
   i                         r
   t                         s,
   h

   s
   n
   o
   w
```

Editor's note: Read panels right to left.

First Place, Shelly Reed Thieman, West Des Moines, IA

Afghan Matches
A Story of Those Arranged, Those Struck

Yasmin washed her clothes
in gasoline, dressed, struck
the last match on a stone.
No longer exotic prey for rape
by extremists who haunt
her missing nose, phantom limb.
I dreamt I became the president.
When I awoke I was a charred beggar in the world.

While her husband shopped
for vegetables, Nagamani
drenched herself with kerosene,
struck the match, shimmied
with flame. Gone the rumors
of liaison with transport worker,
gone the savage quarrels
with husband, in-laws.
May God bring death to village gossips
so the bravest girls will be free of their wagging lips.

Married off to cousin Aziz
at sixteen, Fawzia was beaten
three years by husband and brother.
Marinated in cooking fuel,
she struck the match twice.
Blue burqa and dark hair combusted.
I spilled his white rice on the clean floor.
Old goat stands in the kitchen waving a two by four.

Given in marriage at twelve
as payment for debt, Farzana
handed husband their nine-
month-old daughter. Perfumed
with petrol, she walked outside,
struck the match. Father said
she was not brave enough to do it.
You sold me to an old man, father.
May God destroy your home. I was your only daughter.

Note: The last two lines of each stanza are traditional Landay
poems (syllable-count folk couplets written by Afghan women).

Poetic Globetrotting

This chipped bookshelf circumnavigates the globe
in one single dusty span: Fernando Pessoa
links arms with Nikki Giovanni,
years of quarterly journals get cozy with the past and future
as gallivanting poets dog-ear each others' pages,
their covers spreading a contagion of creativity
from one end of the shelf to the other.
Absolutely no one wants to wash the ink off their hands.
In this confined space, it's impossible to avoid cross-contamination.
Billy Collins complains of the poor legroom, but then again,
he's sharing the corner with e.e.cummings and his entire collected works.
Maggie Smith fares better, being propped between svelte Romanians
and someone's free-gift-with-purchase.
Everyone is jealous of Sarah Lindsay and her own dedicated wing,
Lucia Perillo and other esteemed poets of disability are
extremely accessible, given places of honor.
It's a beautiful sight, the way they lean on each other,
support the weak, refuse to crumble in the face of infrequent readings.
After the convention, dusty, cross-pollinated,
poets stand in silence at attention,
rapt in layers of internal splendor.

Third Place, Lisa Baldwin, Grants Pass, OR

Poetry Is a Country

Only Poetry can make the world whole
Walls go up and borders close
But a poem won't stay barred for long
Fly over Dig deeper Come home

Walls divide and close more than borders
Alliances come untied and drift
Fly over Dig deeper Come home
I'll be working here where we started

Friends come undone and drift
And it's hard to know what to say
I'm working here where we started
Weaving lines to find my way

It's hard to know what to say
Yet a poem won't stay penned for long
Weaving lines as roads leading home
Only Poetry will make the world whole

First Place, Lorraine Jeffery, Orem, UT

Bathtub Lake

Where does bathtub water go? I asked
    as Mama dried my head.
Down the pipes, to a faraway place.
    That's what my mother said.

I thought about my question as I
    listened to the water drip,
but I answered it myself when Dad took
    me and Jake on a fishing trip.

I caught a fish but the pole was heavy
    and I left Dad and Jake,
and as I walked through the tall weeds,
    I found a bathtub lake.

It smelled awful stinky and wasn't
    where I'd want to play,
but when I saw the brownish soap suds,
    I knew it right away.

There were globs of peanut butter that
    washed off some kid's face,
and there were green grass stains and dirt
    and bugs all over the place.

But Dad just shook his head, even when
    I showed him the leftover soap.
This isn't where the bath water goes? I asked
    He rolled his eyes and said, *Nope.*

But grownups don't know everything.
    I know that for heaven's sakes,
and dirty bath water must go somewhere.
    Why not in bathtub lakes?

Second Place, Doris Jones, Madison, MS

Hummingbird Hoedown

Hummers power
from flow'r to flow'r,
chip and churr . . .
whip and whurr!

Hummingbirds
fall in line . . .
sometimes dance in
double time!

Daisy-doe,
'round they go . . .
zooming past,
moving fast!

Something bright
catches light.
Red and sweet . . .
attention wanes . . .
Let's eat!

All abuzz . . .
zip and dip,
dip and zip.

Flitting, flighting,
so much fussing,
so much fighting!

Hummingbirds hoedown,
'bout till sundown;
when the showdown
s l o w s   d o w n.

Then hummers,
all meek-beeked,
dare to share . . .
then peep,
fall *fast* asleep.

Third Place, Patricia Barnes, Wyandotte, MI

My Pet, My Pet, Whatever Shall It Be?

A kitten or a puppy or a fish,
the choice was up to me my mama said
At last I would receive my birthday wish.
A zoo of critters danced inside my head.

A Saint Bernard was big enough to ride,
a Siamese would have blue eyes like me,
I could not choose no matter how I tried.
What about fish that sparkle like the sea?

The man who ran the pet store said he knew
the perfect pet for any little kid
and as he spoke a bright green parrot flew
and landed on my head. It really did.

That's how I learned a lesson, oh so true.
You do not choose the pet, it chooses you.

First Place, Carolyn Evans Campbell, Evergreen, CO

Child of the Prairie

I am a Child of the Prairie
wearing the heavy hob-nailed boots
of my dead brother
and the shape of his foot.

I roll, unheeded, with tumbleweeds,
tornados, and buffalo stampedes,
across the plains, dance
with dust devils as the eagle cuts the sky.

I wear a burnt face like a giant sunflower
always facing the sun as I walk west.
I plod through Wyoming wind, a weary ox
stumbling into waterless *arroyos*.

I hide my face in the shadow
of my sunbonnet as I bury my child
in a nowhere place.
Under a vast, night sky, I listen
to the hungry howl of coyotes.

My hair, dry as sage, tangles
with a bluebird's nest; sometimes
meadowlarks' songs and red sunsets
fill my heart, my prayers.

Child of the Prairie, you cannot skip
in your brother's boots heavy with dirt clods.
Though you step lightly over dry buffalo grass,
imagining your small foot in pink satin slippers,
you cannot change who you are.

Remember, you are ancient,
built from the bones of beasts,

red clay, sun-bleached sage,
rolling tumbleweeds, violent storms,
torrents of flood water roaring
through your veins.
You will always be a Child of the Prairie.

Second Place, Deborah Goschy, Eagle Lake, MN

A Letter from the Prairie 1878

"Dear Mother and Father,
The wind never stops blowing on the prairie,
a 'Prairie Poltergeist' that rattles the windows
and sets the timbers creaking.
It seems to talk to me," she wrote.

> Her pen scratched against the paper but in her ears
> she heard the music of the wind on the prairie grass,
> a sonata of rustles, moans, and murmurs.

"The wind embraces me as if it has been lonely,
presses a breezy hand hard against my back and tugs
on my skirts, whispers 'Come play with me,' and engages
me in clothesline battles, a tug of war with wet, white sheets,
fills them with air and they belly like the sails of a great ship.
Sometimes I vow that I could almost feel the cool kiss of ocean
spray, but I fear that it is only my own wishful thinking.
Just a dream of water on dry land."

> Or Prairie Madness, she thought, looking at her words.
> Mother will wonder what is ailing me.
> She paused before committing the next words to paper.

"We still have the drought here."

> She pondered the hopes that she and Hiram cherished,
> that God would reward them for stepping out in faith,
> that rain would follow the plow, as they had followed
> an advertisement: bold letters on bright yellow paper
> that proclaimed AMERICA'S GARDEN OF EDEN!
> Words that promised a harvest of plenty.

"Never have I prayed so hard for the sound of thunder,
for breath out of the west heavy with the scent of coming rain,
as I have in this place of teeming land and abundant sky,

exposed to the Eye of God. Surely He knows where to find us,"
she continued, wincing at her desperation, her blasphemy.

She dabbed at her eyes with her handkerchief.

"I think of you all daily, and pray that you are well."
"All my love,   Katrina"

Third Place, Christine Irving, Denton, TX

The Cowgirl and the Raven

Cowgirl dreaming, flying high
Raven watching, standing by.
Worlds to travel Here and There
Above, Below, Earth and Air.
Raven cawing, "Follow me!
Doors to open, sights to see!"

Cowgirl nightmares
fight or flee?
Ley lines, patterns
where's the key?
How unravel
tangled knots
forgotten stories
useless plots?

Teton mountains
shining bright,
snaking rivers,
starry nights.
Raven trapped
in sticky thread
clicks his talons
bobs his head,
tears at strands
that seek to hold
chooses freedom
dares be bold.

Cowgirl dreaming, sings a song,
yodels, cackles loud and long.
Wipes her face of snot and tears
rids herself of guilt and fears,
flaps her arms, flying high,
Raven watches, standing by.

First Place, Terry Jude Miller, Richmond, TX

Truck

too poor to afford store-bought toys
he made a truck of canning-jar lids,
nails, and a discarded scrap of wood

he hauled acorns, pinecones,
fallen pomegranates around the knotty knees
of grandfather oaks

drove stickman soldiers to the frontlines
to bring freedom
to the farmhouse

at night he parked his prize
under the porch next
to his sister's mud-pie pans

the next day he'd be
her delivery man

Second Place, Steven Leitch, West Jordan, UT

The Master Gardener

She was a master gardener and as any gardener knows,
it's time to till in early spring to make a garden grow.

The furrows must be deep and straight and clear of noxious weeds,
for the skills of master gardeners are where they plant their seeds.

Too deep the seeds will miss the light, too shallow wash away.
A gardener knows exactly where the seeds will root and stay.

When as each plant begins its life from seed to sprout as such,
it needs the knowing gentle hand of a master gardener's touch.

Her gardens always blossomed with bloom and fruited yield,
there never was a season's past that showed an empty field.

Now blooms her finest garden, five sons who stand today,
she knew to plant exactly where her seeds would root and stay.

She tended them as gardeners do with firm but gentle care,
not a noxious weed among them, for if there was, beware.

She was a master gardener, it is sad to see her go,
but now there is a field above, for her to till and sow.

For He who calls us children, will raise her from her bounds,
to be the Master's gardener, in Heaven's fertile grounds.

Third Place, Marilyn Huntman Giese, Aurora, IL

Message from the Midnight Moon

Sitting at my kitchen table,
  waiting for cookies to finish baking,
I look up and see shining through my window
  a bright midnight moon,
its crescent shape like a hammock
  with a lazy dreamer in its curved pouch.

My heart skips a beat
  at the unexpected brilliance.
I swear the shimmering light filling the room
  is my husband's smile reaching out to me.

  Perhaps the brownies in the oven
   brought him near tonight.
  The aroma always transported him to my side,
   with his hand ready for the first warm morsel.

First Place, Dave Harvey, Talent, OR

The Color of Deep Water, Mid-Pacific

[Aboard *USS Okanogan,* (APA-220), March, 1961]

Rhumb-lining west in convoy,
   Pearl Harbor to Buckner Bay,
sunny morning,
I look off the bridge wing,
down into the water.

We're fifteen hundred miles from Pearl,
   well past Midway Island,
no land to starboard for three thousand miles—
nothing to port until you hit Antarctica—
and the water looks black.

We're steaming above the Abyssal Plain;
soundings show three thousand fathoms
   and more—
we're as high off the ground
   as DC-Sixes used to fly.

And I look down,
   gaze into three and a half miles

of sunlight-drowning,
tons-of-pressure-per-square-inch,
abyssal,

black

black

water.

Second Place, K. Hamblen, Baton Rouge, LA

Maiden Voyage of an Iceberg, 400 AD — April 1912

An ice white calf
Dappled with lichen and dozing birds
Breaking from her family, a tightly knit glacier clan
Leaving with a roar and a splash
Taking off on her own, without a plan
Only knowing she craves warmth
Floating South, pulled slowly to her death
Becoming less each day
Large for her age, so much more than seen
Only a hint of size, hiding her girth
Under a skirt of waves
Moving steadily over the centuries
Pulling along a fog of chilled haze
Regal in her destiny, a matron of ice
Frigid, in fact, giving ships the cold shoulder
Floating well ahead of the normal ice pack
She sees it:
Jewels in the moonless Atlantic night
Dots moving from the east
Within a cocoon of its own light
Nothing seen beyond itself
Hidden in the dark, minding her own business
A chill water, a breeze of ice, the only signals sent
To the ship of bedecked fools, tempting limits
She sees it all:
A still moment, a hesitation, then fate
Moving into her
An intrusion, so uncalled for, so impolite
Crushing, whacking along her side
Metal grinding against the home of birds
Sent in crying flight; cracks, fractures, fissures
Water rushing into two fragile shells

Sharing a common fate and then that screaming
She hears it all

She continues South, avoided even by the curious
With a swatch of red paint on her weak side
The mark of Cain
Her majesty gone within the year
Last seen, a sliver of melting ice.

Third Place, Jon Sebba, Murray, UT

Surge of Affection

Awake before dawn,
Sea turns sleepily,
brushes Rock's side.
She slumbers, immovable.

Sea bestirs himself,
raises a wave on one elbow
to caress Rock's flank,
nestles against her base.

Rock sighs softly,
as Sea bathes her feet
in warm water, runs rivulets
along her shoulders.

Sea envelops her,
strokes the kelp growing on her
crown, runs white-frothed fingers
along Rock's inundated crevices.

Sea splashes, agitates
foam on her cheeks,
surges against her,
moves her on their bed of sand.

As the sun rises
to kiss the sober clouds,
Sea's waves crash higher,
bathing Rock in saltiness.

They cling together until
the tide turns, recedes,
energy subsides,
docile and spent.

Rock basks in sun,
imperturbable, warmed.
A languid Sea
laps at her toes.

First Place, Barbara Blanks, Garland, TX

Guardian of Lochinvar Plantation

Pontotoc, Mississippi

(a Split Gloss)

As I was going up the stair
I met a man who wasn't there!
   —Hughes Mearns, "Antigonish"

A being breathing thoughtful breath,
a traveler between life and death
   — William Wordsworth,
      "She Was a Phantom of Delight"

As I was going up the stair
reality was torn askew.
I'm not insane—but hitherto
I've never had an impromptu
or unexpected rendezvous
as I was going up the stair.

I met a man who wasn't there!
Where did he come from? What a shock!
Did someone leave the front door lock
unlatched? I didn't hear a knock.
I fear I'll be a laughingstock—
I met a man who wasn't there.

A being breathing thoughtful breath—
I bet it's Uncle Eb, the slave,
who cared for Lochinvar—he gave
his all to guard the place, to stave
off prowlers—from beyond the grave.
A being breathing thoughtful breath,

a traveler between life and death—
a loyal man, who'll never go.
His ghostly form moves to and fro,
and roams the property, a glow
like lantern light from long ago—
a traveler between life and death.

Second Place, Elizabeth Horrocks, Wilmslow, Cheshire, UK

Breaking Through

(Shakespearean Sonnet)

Perhaps this room once had a simple door,
but shaping and reshaping through the years
left it abandoned, cut off, known no more,
its cloaking darkness full of hopes or fears.
And then in our own "refurb" we knocked through
the barrier of brick and shone a light
in that dark space, and through the dust, shapes grew
and they revealed to our astonished sight
the sad detritus of a former life,
not worth the rescuing—or did they mean
to hide that chair, that gown, that bowl, that knife?
Then in the air we heard a fading keen:
an echoing voice confined for years, distressed,
now free to leave and finally find rest.

Third Place, Grace Diane Jessen, Glenwood, UT

Haunted

The old house sits on a corner lot
at the western edge of town;
the adobe walls are patched with brick
to keep them from falling down.

The window frames are of weathered wood
which surrounds small, smoky panes,
and the porch once trimmed with gingerbread
now sags and rots from the rains.

The last to live in this forlorn place
was a tough old man named Jack.
When he died, his son wouldn't sell the lot,
but he left and never came back.

Some people claim they have passed the house
on a dreary autumn day
and they saw the dingy curtains move,
pulled aside by a hand of gray.

Yet others swear they have seen the form
of a woman through the glass;
she was dressed in white and turned to stare
at those who were walking past.

When cold winds moan through the leafless trees
that now guard this lonely spot,
some fancy they hear a mournful cry,
a wailing from who knows what.

Can they be true, all these tales now told
of the tall, old house? Or could
it be Imagination's ghost
that paces those floors of wood?

First Place, Meredith R. Cook, Blue Earth, MN

Achieving Détente,
or, A Lesson for Xenophobic Warmongers
(Irish Sonnet)

The dog gripes of intruders on the beach.
His muscled golden chest strains at the rope
that tethers weathered wood deck to his leash,
keeps him from bounding down where two hounds lope.

The two small dachshunds that his eyes can scope
are frolicking on sand that wraps the lake,
but by *his* cabin, not three down the slope
of shoreline, where they're owned. Growls make him shake.

He needs to meet these strangers. Should rope break
he'd hurtle down like rockfall from the sky,
descend, confront the liberties they take,
declare this land-plot's his; they can't go by!

Yet when he's loosed from bondage, swoops from high
on hill, accosts them, all sniff: no blows fly.

Second Place, Emory D. Jones, Iuka, MS

Sacred Music

(a Gloss)

Methinks it should have been impossible
Not to love all things in a world so filled;
Where the breeze warbles and the mute still air
Is Music slumbering on her instrument.
—Samuel Taylor Coleridge, "The Eolian Harp"

Methinks it should have been impossible
Not to feel the rhythm of the spheres,
The joyous music of the Lord's which still
In undertones so permeates our ears—
Methinks it should have been impossible

Not to love all things in a world so filled
With symphonies of His created score
With chords so firm and harmony that's trilled
By every living thing that we adore—
Not to love all things in a world so filled

Where the breeze warbles, and the mute still air
Is but the pause before the music swells
Again in great crescendo of our prayer
Of praise to Him from everyone who dwells
Where the breeze warbles, and the mute still air

Is Music slumbering on her instrument
In dreams of the eternal song to Him
Who orchestrates the harmonies He meant
To elevate our souls—our silent hymn
Is Music slumbering on her instrument.

Third Place, Kathy Lohrum Cotton, Anna, IL

At the Psychiatric Museum

*Pica: Abnormal desire to eat
substances not normally eaten.*
—Merriam-Webster

The pica art is a collection
of small, everyday items,
the tour guide tells us,
pointing out a shadow box
of artistically arranged pieces:

the threaded-edge saltshaker top
with pierced patterns,
a breakfast spoon's shapely handle,
pearly shirt buttons, smooth orbs
of beads and ball bearings,
sharp-tipped metal lengths
of nails, tacks and screws,
the guarded prick of safety pins.

I imagine the stunned surgeon
removing, one by one,
these 1,446 ordinary objects
secreted inside a patient's body,
bequeathed by a last torn breath
and now displayed at
the museum in St. Joe.

The guide tells us
that another pica patient
swallowed a Timex.
It passed, still ticking.

First Place, Bianca Singelstad, Lake Mills, IA

Floating

They only see our failures.
Our faults.
They watch our muddy footprints,
That were tracked through the house.
They blame our failures on our cell phones,
Or laptops,
Or PlayStations,
Without realizing what else we can do.
Without seeing every success.
They miss the moments that matter
Because of clothes that we forgot to fold,
Or dishes we didn't put away.
They yell so often that it's normal,
Like a nightmare of a song,
To the point where success doesn't matter.
We hide our stories,
The solos we have,
The games we start in,
Because yesterday you said you didn't love us.

We aren't asking for perfection,
Because we aren't perfect, either.
All we want is love,
Everlasting love.
We need those little reminders that you care,
That life is more than chores and yelling.
That life is about being adventurous,
And floating in the moment.
And we'll try to remember the same about you.
That you need love, too.

Second Place, Sarah Meeks, LIttle Rock, AR

Something Like a Story

The spine creeks softly,
My fingers run across the smooth paper
As if they can absorb the words into my blood
To create the thrum of excited anticipation
I feel in my bones.

Breaths of surprise and squeals of joy
Mingle with tears for people who aren't real,
But that means nothing to me
As my eyes scan the page faster than a flash of lightning.

I have left the real world.
Everything is real and nothing is
In this imaginary place.
Even the reminders of reality,
Like the minty explosion
and the scent of ink-filled pages
That whisper inside of me,
Do nothing to bring me out of my bliss.

I don't hear silence.
I hear battle cries
And stories that begin with
Once upon a time;
Silence does not exist in my mind.
I live
And I die
A thousand times over,
But each life ends
With the solemn close of a book,
Like the sealing of a casket.
Until I find a new tale to engulf me.

Third Place, Megan Johnson, Ely, IA

Number One on My To Do List

I cannot express how much work I have
None of it's complete
and I'm running on five hours of sleep.
Gusts of wind hit the window
as I struggle
with my workload.
I erase two sentences
right after I complete one.
I wish I could rely on coffee
but it's extremely late.
I'll say I will never wait
until the last minutes
as soon as I'm done.
But I guess procrastination
will always be number one
on my "To Do" list.

First Place, Megan Goughnour, Polk City, IA

Family

Just
When
You thought
Life couldn't get any harder, with troubles raining down,
Family becomes an umbrella,
Blocking them out.

Second Place, Laney Pearson, Denver, CO

Addiction

Unable to stop
Helpless to what I've caught
Surrogate life forever
See you in heaven, my lover

Negligent to the truth
Engrossed in my youth
Happiness for a second
I'll die soon, I reckon

Unstable for existence
Everyone keeps their distance
The old me; I've killed off
I surmise, an unfair trade-off

For yes I accepted
Overlooked that my life would be intercepted
To my dear enslavement
That I've got myself caught in

Roped around me
Never allowing me to flee
I've been beaten by this illness
Until I feel a certain stillness

Third Place, Emma Paris, Putney, VT

Did You Know, America

Dear America,

what's wrong America,
not what you expected—
do your people still love you
when bombs are effective?
What's wrong America,
some second thoughts—
guess that's what happens
in the "big melting pot."
What's wrong America,
do our protests annoy you—
did you know singing and
yelling were on the menu?
What's wrong America,
eating disorder—
maybe now you can relate
to the children at the border?
What's wrong America,
are we a disgrace?
All we're trying to do is
save the whole human race.
What's wrong America,
are your children revolting?
Guess that's what happens when
the whole world starts smoking.
Oh America, all we want is some peace,
ya' know, it's real hard to get
when the whole world's for lease.
America, won't you listen to us,
please take note that love is enough.
Freedom, stars on flags and eagles,
please catch up on the century;
no human being is illegal.

First Place, Julia Irish, Lakewood, CO

The Shadow

Human shadow slides,
Light floods its path with beauty.
The soul will follow.

Second Place, Jack Hillman, Ames, IA

Frank

There once was a cat named Frank
He liked to take fish out of the tank
He ate the fish
Off of a dish
He was oh so very dank

Third Place, Laura Austin, McHenry, KY

The Rose

for Mom on Mother's Day, 2019

You are the thorn of the rose
and you're filled with love.
I am the flower of the rose
filled with love for you.
The stem of the rose is the pathway to our love.

Abernathy, Charlotte; Ashland, OR, #23, HM 2

Ahearn, James F.; Rochester, MI, #35, HM 3

Ajami, Jocelyn; Chicago, IL, #14, HM 6

Ajami, Jocelyn; Chicago, IL, #29, HM 6

Alexander, Becky; Cambridge, Ontario Canada, #49, HM 2

Altshul, Laura; New Haven, CT, #32, HM 1

Austin-Hill, Suzanne; Ruskin, FL, #21, HM 4

Bailey, Karen Kay; Blanchard, OK, #23, HM 5

Bailey, Karen Kay; Blanchard, OK, #40, HM 5

Bailey, Rebecca L.; Grangeville, ID, #11, HM 1

Bailey, Valerie Martin; San Antonio, TX, #7, HM 3

Baldwin, Lisa; Grants Pass, OR, #17, HM 5

Baldwin, Lisa; Grants Pass, OR, #18, HM 1

Balph, Martha H.; Millville, UT, #13, HM 3

Balph, Martha H.; Millville, UT, #36, HM 5

Balph, Martha H.; Millville, UT, #48, HM 5

Balph, Martha H.; Millville, UT, #50, HM 3

Banks, Linda; Mesquite, TX, #21, HM 6

Banks, Linda; Mesquite, TX, #29, HM 4

Banks, Linda; Mesquite, TX, #38, HM 3

Banks, Linda; Mesquite, TX, #46, HM 1

Barker, Crystal; Los Angeles, CA, #27, HM 7

Barker, Crystal; Los Angeles, CA, #33, HM 5

Barnes, Patricia; Wyandotte, MI, #13, HM 1

Barnes, Patricia; Wyandotte, MI, #20, HM 5

Barnes, Patricia; Wyandotte, MI, #3, HM 7

Barnes, Patricia; Wyandotte, MI, #31, HM 7

Barnes, Patricia; Wyandotte, MI, #43, HM 2

Barnes, Patricia; Wyandotte, MI, #46, HM 3

Barnes, Patricia; Wyandotte, MI, #48, HM 7

Barney, V. Kimball; Kaysville, UT, #3, HM 4

Barney, V. Kimball; Kaysville, UT, #33, HM 7

Barney, V. Kimball; Kaysville, UT, #37, HM 7

Bell, Jean; Evergreen, CO, #12, HM 2

Bennett, Jonathan; Lakeland, TN, #16, HM 2

Blackwell, Shirley; Los Lunas, NM, #21, HM 7

Blackwell, Shirley; Los Lunas, NM, #41, HM 3

Blackwell, Shirley; Los Lunas, NM, #9, HM 7

Blanks, Barbara; Garland, TX, #12, HM 4

Blanks, Barbara; Garland, TX, #15, HM 2

Blanks, Barbara; Garland, TX, #36, HM 3

Blanks, Barbara; Garland, TX, #38, HM 5

Blanks, Barbara; Garland, TX, #5, HM 2

Blenheim, Robert E.; Daytona Beach, FL, #14, HM 2

Blenheim, Robert E.; Daytona Beach, FL, #49, HM 7

Blenkush, Micki; St. Cloud, MN, #19, HM 4

Blenkush, Micki; St. Cloud, MN, #31, HM 1

Blenkush, Micki; St. Cloud, MN, #39, HM 6

Blenkush, Micki; St. Cloud, MN, #6, HM 6

Bond, David; Del Rio, TX, #8, HM 1

Bourland, Von S.; Happy, TX, #1, HM 7

Bourland, Von S.; Happy, TX, #22, HM 5

Bourland, Von S.; Happy, TX, #3, HM 1

Bourland, Von S.; Happy, TX, #44, HM 6

Bourland, Von S.; Happy, TX, #7, HM 5

Bourland, Von S.; Happy, TX, #9, HM 3

Breen, Nancy; Loveland, OH, #7, HM 1

Brekke-Kramer, Ed; Fairmont, MN, #7, HM 4

Brown, Markay; St. George, UT, #2, HM 1

Call, Karen; Aurora, CO, #27, HM 4

Campbell, Carolyn Evans; Evergreen, CO, #24, HM 6

Campbell, Carolyn Evans; Evergreen, CO, #43, HM 1

Campbell, Susan; Mansfield, TX, #24, HM 1

Carlson, Maxine; Iowa City, IA, #22, HM 7

Casto, Pamelyn; De Cordova, TX, #39, HM 1

Chambers, Susan; Mankato, MN, #17, HM 1

Chambers, Susan; Mankato, MN, #18, HM 7

Chambers, Susan; Mankato, MN, #46, HM 5

Chapman, Aubrey; Osage, IA, #52, HM 7

Chisholm, Alison; Southport, UK, #11, HM 6

Chisholm, Alison; Southport, UK, #30, HM 6

Chisholm, Alison; Southport, UK, #33, HM 1

Chisholm, Alison; Southport, UK, #44, HM 2

Chisholm, Alison; Southport, UK, #49, HM 1

Collins, Trysten; Ames, IA, #53, HM 2

Conklin, Joshua; Amherst, NH, #44, HM 1

Conklin, Joshua; Amherst, NH, #47, HM 1

Conklin, Joshua; Amherst, NH, #48, HM 4

Conklin, Joshua; Amherst, NH, #8, HM 3

Cook, Crystie; Sandy, UT, #30, HM 2

Cook, Nancy; St. Paul, MN, #2, HM 4

Cook, Nancy; St. Paul, MN, #26, HM 2

Coppock, John W.; Tuttle, OK, #10, HM 2

Coppock, John W.; Tuttle, OK, #30, HM 1

Coppock, John W.; Tuttle, OK, #37, HM 1

Cordaro, Jin; Jackson, NJ, #1, HM 4

Cotton, Kathy Lohrum; Anna, IL, #22, HM 1

Cotton, Kathy Lohrum; Anna, IL, #27, HM 1

Cotton, Kathy Lohrum; Anna, IL, #32, HM 3

Cotton, Kathy Lohrum; Anna, IL, #8, HM 2

Craig, Summer; North Little Rock, AR, #51, HM 2

Daubenspeck; Susan, Corpus Christi, TX, #34, HM 7

Davidson; Marc, Daytona Beach, FL, #34, HM 1

Davidson; Marc, Daytona Beach, FL, #9, HM 4

Davis, Robert V.; West Haven, UT, #40, HM 1

Dembosky, Doris; Penrose, CO, #19, HM 7

Dembosky, Doris, Penrose, CO, #25, HM 2

Denham, Gail; Sunriver, OR, #26, HM 6

Denham, Gail; Sunriver, OR, #35, HM 2

Denham, Gail; Sunriver, OR, #37, HM 5

Dohlman, Marjorie; Riceville, IA, #45, HM 6

Donovan, Charmaine Pappas; Brainerd, MN, #12, HM 7

Donovan, Charmaine Pappas; Brainerd, MN, #14, HM 4

Donovan, Charmaine Pappas; Brainerd, MN, #6, HM 7

Durmon, Pat; Norfolk, AR, #25, HM 5

Durmon, Pat; Norfolk, AR, #6, HM 5

Escoubas, Michael; Bloomington, IL, #10, HM 1

Feenstra, Judith; Maple Lake, MN, #13, HM 7

Feenstra, Judith; Maple Lake, MN, #35, HM 7

Feenstra, Judith; Maple Lake, MN, #39, HM 5

Felt, Geraldine G.; Layton, UT, #26, HM 3

Finnegan, Brenda Brown; Ocean Springs, MS, #48, HM 2

Firmage, Charles K.; Eagle Pass, TX, #17, HM 7

Ford, Barbara, Poncha Springs, CO, #10, HM 7

Freytag, Janice L.; Souderton, PA, #21, HM 3

Freytag, Janice L.; Souderton, PA, #39, HM 3

Freytag, Janice L.; Souderton, PA, #43, HM 5

Freytag, Janice L.; Souderton, PA, #7, HM 2

Funke, Barbara J.; St. George, UT, #41, HM 5

Fusco, Tony; West Haven, CT, #18, HM 4

Giese, Marilyn Huntman; Aurora, IL, #42, HM 6

Gipson, Sara; Scott, AR, #23, HM 3

Gipson, Sara; Scott, AR, #47, HM 7

Glancy, Diane; Gainsville, TX, #48, HM 1

Gordon, Peter; Orlando, FL, #5, HM 7

Gordon, Peter; Orlando, FL, #8, HM 5

Gorrell, Dena R.; Edmond, OK, #21, HM 2

Gorrell, Dena R.; Edmond, OK, #5, HM 5

Goschy, Deborah; Eagle Lake, MN, #33, HM 3

Greaver, Alliyah; Yankton, SD, #14, HM 1

Guinn, Fay; Jonesboro, AR, #45, HM 2

Haines, Alice; Auburn, ME, #41, HM 7

Hamblen, K.; Baton Rouge, LA, #1, HM 2

Hansen, Laura; Little Falls, MN, #24, HM 4

Hardesty, Jerri; Brierfield, AL, #33, HM 2

Hardesty, Jerri; Brierfield, AL, #45, HM 3

Hardesty, Jerri; Brierfield, AL, #6, HM 1

Harvey, Dave; Talent, OR, #28, HM 5

Hasan, Omair; Toledo, OH, #11, HM 4

Hasan, Omair; Toledo, OH, #2, HM 7

Hasan, Omair; Toledo, OH, #31, HM 3

Hasan, Omair; Toledo, OH, #50, HM 6

Hoffman, Janice; Williamsburg, VA, #31, HM 4

Honeycutt, Beth; Denton, TX, #44, HM 4

Hope, M.E.; O'Fallon, IL, #7, HM 6

Horrocks, Elizabeth; Wilmslow, Cheshire, UK, #41, HM 1

Hughes, Betsy M.; Dayton, OH, #19, HM 6

Hughes, Betsy M.; Dayton, OH, #36, HM 4

Hughes, Betsy M.; Dayton, OH, #42, HM 7

Hurzeler, Richard P.; Tyler, TX, #20, HM 7

Irish, Amy Wray; Lakewood, CO, #13, HM 5

Irish, Amy Wray; Lakewood, CO, #41, HM 4

Irving, Christine; Denton, TX, #29, HM 1

Jacks, Terrie; Ballwin, MO, #17, HM 6

Jeffery, Lorraine; Orem, UT, #10, HM 6

Jeffery, Lorraine; Orem, UT, #12, HM 5

Jeffery, Lorraine; Orem, UT, #18, HM 2

Jeffery, Lorraine; Orem, UT, #41, HM 2

Jennings, Mimi; Saint Paul, MN, #19, HM 1

Jepson-Gilbert; Anita, Westminster, CO, #18, HM 3

Jepson-Gilbert; Anita; Westminster, CO, #24, HM 7

Jepson-Gilbert; Anita; Westminster, CO, #36, HM 1

Jepson-Gilbert; Anita; Westminster, CO, #42, HM 4

Jessen, Grace Diane; Glenwood, UT, #16, HM 4

Jessen, Grace Diane; Glenwood, UT, #21, HM 1

Jessen, Grace Diane; Glenwood, UT, #38, HM 4

Jessen, Grace Diane; Glenwood, UT, #46, HM 4

Johnson, Carlton; Winter Park, FL, #48, HM 3

Johnson, Julie; Norwalk, IA, #8, HM 6

Jones, Doris; Madison, MS, #17, HM 3

Jones, Doris; Madison, MS, #31, HM 6

Jones, Emory D.; Iuka, MS, #35, HM 5

Jones, Libby; Berea, KY, #2, HM 5

Jones, Shelley; Johnston, IA, #20, HM 3

Jones, Shelley; Johnston, IA, #45, HM 7

Juettner, Carie; Austin, TX, #25, HM 1

Kentwortz, Ravitte; Louisville, CO, #11, HM 7

Kentwortz, Ravitte; Louisville, CO, #46, HM 6

Koch, Patricia Jo; Oklahoma City, OK, #49, HM 4

Kolp, Laurie; Beaumont, TX, #2, HM 2

Kolp, Laurie; Beaumont, TX, #24, HM 5

Krotz, Anita; Salt Lake City, UT, #15, HM 3

Krotz, Anita; Salt Lake City, UT, #30, HM 4

Krotz, Anita; Salt Lake City, UT, #44, HM 5

Krotz, Anita; Salt Lake City, UT, #49, HM 3

Kyveryga, Sophie; Ames, IA, #53, HM 1

L'Herisson, Catherine; Garland, TX, #10, HM 4

L'Herisson, Catherine; Garland, TX, #25, HM 4

L'Herisson, Catherine; Garland, TX, #34, HM 3

L'Herisson, Catherine; Garland, TX, #5, HM 4

L'Herisson, Catherine; Garland, TX, #8, HM 4

La Rocca, Lynda; Salida, CO, #2, HM 6

La Rocca, Lynda; Salida, CO, #22, HM 3

La Rocca, Lynda; Salida, CO, #23, HM 4

La Rocca, Lynda; Salida, CO, #29, HM 3

Leitch, Steven; West Jordan, UT, #11, HM 5

Leitch, Steven; West Jordan, UT, #28, HM 2

Leitch, Steven; West Jordan, UT, #3, HM 3

Leitch, Steven; West Jordan, UT, #43, HM 6

Little, Tommy; Brandon, MS, #29, HM 7

Little, Tommy; Brandon, MS, #42, HM 3

Lowe, Isabell; Sheldahl, IA, #52, HM 3

Lyons, Maurice G.; Mansfield, OH, #25, HM 6

Magee, Mary Beth; Poplarville, MS, #20, HM 6

Mahan, Budd Powell; Dallas, TX, #20, HM 1

Mahan, Budd Powell; Dallas, TX, #24, HM 3

Mahan, Budd Powell; Dallas, TX, #30, HM 7

Mahan, Budd Powell; Dallas, TX, #34, HM 2

Mahan, Budd Powell; Dallas, TX, #4, HM 7

Mahan, Budd Powell; Dallas, TX, #40, HM 2

Mahan, Budd Powell; Dallas, TX, #44, HM 3

Mahan, Budd Powell; Dallas, TX, #9, HM 2

McCann, Janet; College Station, TX, #16, HM 3

McCann, Janet; College Station, TX, #4, HM 2

McCarthy, Lavern Spencer; Blair, OK, #13, HM 6

McCarthy, Lavern Spencer; Blair, OK, #22, HM 4

McCarthy, Lavern Spencer; Blair, OK, #30, HM 3

McCarthy, Lavern Spencer; Blair, OK, #35, HM 4

McCarthy, Lavern Spencer; Blair, OK, #39, HM 4

McCarthy, Lavern Spencer; Blair, OK, #40, HM 3

McCarthy, Lavern Spencer; Blair, OK, #45, HM 5

McCarthy, Lavern Spencer; Blair, OK, #48, HM 6

McCarthy, Lavern Spencer; Blair, OK, #50, HM 5

McCune, BF; Denver, CO, #8, HM 7

McCutcheon, Jade Rosina; Salem, OR, #32, HM 5

McDowell, Joy; Springfield, OR, #15, HM 6

McDowell, Joy; Springfield, OR, #16, HM 1

McDowell, Joy; Springfield, OR, #41, HM 6

McDowell, Joy; Springfield, OR, #47, HM 2

McDowell, Joy; Springfield, OR, #6, HM 4

McKernan, Llewellyn; New Smyrna Beach, FL, #16, HM 6

McKernan, Llewellyn; New Smyrna Beach, FL, #28, HM 7

McPherson, John; Searcy, AR, #46, HM 2

Miller, Terry Jude; Richmond, TX, #2, HM 3

Miller, Terry Jude; Richmond, TX, #6, HM 3

Million, Marlene; Noblesville, IN, #45, HM 4

Moellers, Kate; LIttle Rock, AR, #51, HM 5

Montague, Kolette; Centerville, UT, #19, HM 2

Montague, Kolette; Centerville, UT, #23, HM 6

Montague, Kolette; Centerville, UT, #26, HM 5

Montague, Kolette; Centerville, UT, #7, HM 7

Moran, Catherine; Little Rock, AR, #30, HM 5

Moran, Catherine; Little Rock, AR, #40, HM 6

Morris, Wilda; Bolingbrook, IL, #15, HM 1

Morris, Wilda; Bolingbrook, IL, #26, HM 4

Morse, Carmel; Lima, OH, #23, HM 1

Morse, Carmel; Lima, OH, #33, HM 4

Mortenson, Virginia; Des Moines, IA, #22, HM 6

Mortenson, Virginia; Des Moines, IA, #43, HM 3

Mortenson, Virginia; Des Moines, IA, #50, HM 2

Mounsey, Pauline; Sun City West, AZ, #37, HM 2

Murphy, Sheila; Portland, CT, #17, HM 2

Nelson-Bradley, Jackson; Davenport, IA, #51, HM 3

Nusbaum, Olivia; Denver, CO, #52, HM 4

Olson, Hailey; Sandborn, IA, #52, HM 2

Opsahl, Polly; Oscoda, MI, #5, HM 1

Panowitsch, Henry; Mankato, MN, #25, HM 3

Panowitsch, Henry; Mankato, MN, #50, HM 1

Pashley, Jenna; Richmond, TX, #4, HM 5

Patton, Dennis R.; Alexander, AR, #34, HM 5

Patton, Dennis R.; Alexander, AR, #38, HM 1

Patton, Dennis R.; Alexander, AR, #42, HM 1

Payne, Linda R.; Fairfield, OH, #38, HM 7

Phillips, Christina; Orlando, FL, #43, HM 4

Picklesimer, Jeani M.; Ashland, KY, #40, HM 7

Pucciani, Donna; Wheaton, IL, #1, HM 6

Pucciani, Donna; Wheaton, IL, #13, HM 2

Pucciani, Donna; Wheaton, IL, #19, HM 5

Pucciani, Donna; Wheaton, IL, #28, HM 6

Pucciani, Donna; Wheaton, IL, #35, HM 6

Pucciani, Donna; Wheaton, IL, #36, HM 2

Pucciani, Donna; Wheaton, IL, #42, HM 2

Puchala, Kathleen; Rockwood, MI, #47, HM 4

Qually, Janet; Memphis, TN, #3, HM 2

Randall, Susan; Orem, UT, #15, HM 4

Reeder, Ray; Albuquerque, NM, #23, HM 7

Reisens, Ana; Sant Just Desvern, Barcelona, #26, HM 1

Ripple, Adrianna; Ft. Wayne, IN, #52, HM 5

Roberts, Nicholis; White Hall, AR, #51, HM 6

Rood, Jennifer; Grants Pass, OR, #45, HM 1

Roth, Isa; Denver, CO, #52, HM 1

Rowley, Jo-Anne; Lafayette, CO, #43, HM 7

Ruttenberg, Crimson; Bedford, IA, #51, HM 7

Salmons, Charles; Pickerington, OH, #22, HM 2

Santer, Rikki; Columbus, OH, #12, HM 6

Santer, Rikki; Columbus, OH, #14, HM 5

Santer, Rikki; Columbus, OH, #4, HM 1

Scherer, Alana; West Des Moines, IA, #51, HM 4

Schinzel, Robert; Highland Village, TX, #39, HM 7

Sebba, Jon; Murray, UT, #27, HM 5

Shack, Elizabeth; Savoy, IL, #9, HM 1

Shavin, Julianza; Fountain, CO, #36, HM 6

Shiver, Joyce; Crystal River, FL, #10, HM 3

Shiver, Joyce; Crystal River, FL, #32, HM 6

Shiver, Joyce; Crystal River, FL, #9, HM 6

Shute, Christian; Cheyenne, WY, #10, HM 5

Simmonds, Nancy; Ft. Wayne, IN, #27, HM 6

Singer, Roger; Old Lyme, CT, #16, HM 7

Snyder, Constance; East Thetford, VT, #1, HM 1

Spangler, Anne Pierre; Lebanon, PA, #19, HM 3

Spears, Michael; Plain City, UT, #46, HM 7

Spears, Michael; Plain City, UT, #47, HM 3

Sprecher, Neve; Ames, IA, #53, HM 3

Staas, Beth; Oak Brook, IL, #35, HM 1

Stanko, Mary Rudbeck; London, Ontario, Canada, #4, HM 4

Stein, Peter; Minneapolis, MN, #12, HM 1

Stein, Peter; Minneapolis, MN, #31, HM 2

Stone, Harvey; Johnson City, TN, #3, HM 6

Strauss, Russell H.; Memphis, TN, #25, HM 7

Strauss, Russell H.; Memphis, TN, #3, HM 5

Strauss, Russell H.; Memphis, TN, #42, HM 5

Strauss, Russell H.; Memphis, TN, #44, HM 7

Strauss, Russell H.; Memphis, TN, #47, HM 6

Strauss, Russell H.; Memphis, TN, #50, HM 7

Strauss, Russell H.; Memphis, TN, #9, HM 5

Stubblefield, Tristan; Marengo, IA, #51, HM 1

Theis, Mary; Talent, OR, #32, HM 4

Thompson, Carol; Tyler, TX, #6, HM 2

Thrushart, Patricia; Clarington, PA, #1, HM 3

Thrushart, Patricia; Clarington, PA, #28, HM 3

Thrushart, Patricia; Clarington, PA, #29, HM 2

Tindall, Mary; Whitehouse, TX, #36, HM 7

Tindall, Mary; Whitehouse, TX, #38, HM 6

Toth Salinas, Lisa; Spring, TX, #15, HM 7

Toth Salinas, Lisa; Spring, TX, #39, HM 2

Treat, Linda; Blue Springs, MS, #20, HM 4

Treat, Linda; Blue Springs, MS, #50, HM 4

Tsvetkov, Alexa; Denver, CO, #52, HM 6

Tyner, Janet; Tyler, TX, #49, HM 6

Underwood, Pat; Colfax, IA, #28, HM 4

Underwood, Pat; Colfax, IA, #34, HM 4

Urban, Tilli; Denver, CO, #37, HM 6

Van Beek, Cheryl; Wesley Chapel, FL, #17, HM 4

Van Beek, Cheryl; Wesley Chapel, FL, #18, HM 5

Van Beek, Cheryl; Wesley Chapel, FL, #24, HM 2

Van Gerven, Claudia; Boulder, CO, #4, HM 3

Visser, Wendy; Cambridge, Ontario, Canada, #13, HM 4

Visser, Wendy; Cambridge, Ontario, Canada, #49, HM 5

Vorreyer, Tina; Westmont, IL, #14, HM 7

Wahl, Mike; Athens, AL, #16, HM 5

Walker, Loretta Diane; Odessa, TX, #32, HM 7

Walters, S. Evan; Lebanon, IN, #27, HM 2

Watson, Janet; Wesley Chapel, FL, #11, HM 3

Watson, Janet; Wesley Chapel, FL, #18, HM 6

Watson, Janet; Wesley Chapel, FL, #40, HM 4

Whitfield, Pam; Rochester, MN, #11, HM 2

Whitney, Tanya R.; Sorrento, LA, #20, HM 2

Whitney, Tanya R.; Sorrento, LA, #32, HM 2

Whitney, Tanya R.; Sorrento, LA, #37, HM 4

Wildrick, Brenda; Fort Morgan, CO, #21, HM 5

Willert, Jeanette; Pell City, AL, #14, HM 3

Willert, Jeanette; Pell City, AL, #27, HM 3

Wilson, Lucille Morgan; Des Moines, IA, #15, HM 5

Wilson, Lucille Morgan; Des Moines, IA, #28, HM 1

Wilson, Lucille Morgan; Des Moines, IA, #31, HM 5

Wilson, Lucille Morgan; Des Moines, IA, #37, HM 3

Wilson, Lucille Morgan; Des Moines, IA, #38, HM 2

Wilson, Lucille Morgan; Des Moines, IA, #47, HM 5

Wilson, Lucille Morgan; Des Moines, IA, #5, HM 6

Wolfe, Lorrie; Windsor, CO, #12, HM 3

Wolfe, Lorrie; Windsor, CO, #33, HM 6

Zannis, Alexandra Moss; Fort Wayne, IN, #29, HM 5

Zannis, Alexandra Moss; Fort Wayne, IN, #34, HM 6

Zimmerman, Elaine; Hamden, CT, #1, HM 5

Zimmerman, Elaine; Hamden, CT, #4, HM 6

Zimmerman, Elaine; Hamden, CT, #5, HM 3